B to Stay B   5 99 net

Raymond E. Sparks, a graduate of the Columbia University Teachers College, was Professor of Physical Education at Springfield College before assuming his present position as Physical Education Specialist with the United States Army. He has coached wrestling and other sports at Wiley, Indiana, High School, Indiana State Teachers College, Columbia University, Wyoming Seminary in Pennsylvania, Springfield College, and for the Navy V-5 Aviation Cadet Training Program. Ray Sparks has been Chairman of the National Collegiate Athletic Association Wrestling Rules Committee, Secretary of the National Amateur Athletic Union Wrestling Committee, a member of the Olympic and National YMCA Wrestling Committees, and is Past President of the American Wrestling Coaches and Officials Association.

WRESTLING
ILLUSTRATED

An Instructional Guide

RAYMOND E. SPARKS

Professor of Physical Education
Springfield College

THE RONALD PRESS COMPANY • NEW YORK

Library of Congress Catalog Card Number: 60-14628
PRINTED IN THE UNITED STATES OF AMERICA

Preface

Originally designed as a syllabus for teachers and students in the wrestling skills and techniques classes at Springfield College, the materials in this book have also been successfully used as a self-teaching manual by wrestlers and coaches throughout the country. The content and its arrangement is the result of many years of experience in developing an effective wrestling program. A student's comment or action in class and discussion with other instructors, coaches, and wrestlers have provided many of the ideas and techniques.

This guide presents the fundamentals of effective wrestling in a progression specifically designed for efficient learning. From the numberless holds, counters, and blocks that constitute skillful wrestling, this book explains and illustrates in detail 65 maneuvers, arranging them in 38 sequences and drills.

The sequences teach the basic wrestling techniques through step-by-step instructions, with each step given in full detail and keyed to an accompanying illustration. In learning the various moves and holds, the wrestler uses them in combinations that progressively develop his skills in a sure and logical manner.

The basic positions and movements are practiced in the warm-up and conditioning activities, and are then followed by the sequences. The holds and maneuvers are also listed in summary according to the usual categories of take-downs, rides, pins, and reversals. An outline for 30 lessons suggests a scheme for individual or class instruction.

The author wishes to express his grateful appreciation to all persons who have shared in the preparation of this book, especially to the students, practice teachers, graduate assistants, and instructors who have participated in the wrestling classes at Springfield College and in the Navy V-5 program. Special acknowledgment is made to the coaches of wrestling who responded to the writer's requests for suggestions and materials. The photographs were taken by Allen Kidoguchi. Demonstrating the various maneuvers with the author is Eric Beardsley, now wrestling coach at Central Washington College of Education. He appears in the white tights. The author is extremely grateful to these men for their patient cooperation and effective work.

RAYMOND E. SPARKS

Springfield, Massachusetts
    August, 1960

Contents

WRESTLING
ILLUSTRATED

1

Introduction

SELECTION OF THE MATERIAL

This course is designed to provide the student with the experience, skills, and understanding necessary for effective participation in wrestling, so far as it is possible to do in 30 lessons. The material for this course has been selected on the basis of the following factors:

1. The student's skill, condition, and interest. (NEEDS)
2. The course objectives. (OBJECTIVES)
3. The prevention of injuries. (SAFETY)
4. The development of a sound and favorable attitude toward the sport. (INTEREST)
5. The rapid development of competence. (PROFICIENCY)

These factors also provide the criteria for the arrangement of the material into a teaching progression which has been extremely effective in accelerating the training of students to become competent performers.

THE CHARACTERISTICS, NEEDS, AND INTERESTS OF THE STUDENTS

At the beginning of each wrestling season, it is assumed that all the students, including the more advanced wrestlers, need the experience of checking through the basic techniques, as presented in this book. After the experienced wrestlers check out, they can then assist as instructors.

The lessons are set up in a progression that emphasizes the development of balance, maneuverability, competent reaction, and confidence. The advanced wrestler as well as the beginner must strive continually to improve these basic qualities which are essential for effective wrestling.

The physical development and condition of the average student is adequate for participation in the work outlined in this course. There is need, however, for further strengthening of the neck muscles and for increasing the flexibility of the trunk, thorax, and shoulder girdle. These developments are emphasized from the very beginning of the course.

1

Students who have competence and experience in other sports can usually maintain a fast pace in the learning progression of this course. Care must be taken, however, not to discourage the skilled performers from other sports by placing them in competitive situations that may embarrass them. Since most wrestlers have an opportunity to teach others, they need a knowledge of methods as well as curriculum content and performing ability in wrestling. In addition they need to have an appreciation of the contribution wrestling makes to the growth and development of the individual.

THE COURSE OBJECTIVES

The objectives for the course arise from the characteristics, needs, and interests of all wrestlers who are training to develop effective skills and teach the sport.

There are two main objectives, with supplementary objectives listed under each, as follows:

1. To develop personal competence for effective participation in wrestling, which includes:
   a. Knowledge of techniques, rules, and strategy of wrestling.
   b. Neuromuscular skill for effective maneuverability, including agility, speed, balance, and flexibility to perform a variety of wrestling maneuvers.
   c. Endurance, strength, and vigor to compete in the class work and the competition.
   d. Appreciation of wrestling as a wholesome developmental and continuing activity for all ages, sizes, and body types of boys and men, including the handicapped.
   e. Appreciation of wrestling as an effective means of self-defense in unarmed combat.
   f. Appreciation of wrestling as contributing to qualities of personal and social behavior, which include self-expression, self-reliance, confidence, initiative, self-discipline, determination, perseverance, courage, regard for rules, and courtesy.

2. To develop professional competencies for effective teaching and administration of amateur wrestling, which includes:
   a. Skill in explaining and demonstrating the wrestling techniques.
   b. Skill in recording matches and in refereeing.
   c. Knowledge of rules, terminology, and strategy.
   d. Knowledge and performing ability in all the activities of the course.
   e. Knowledge of the principles involved in wrestling.
   f. A conviction that wrestling is a very important activity in providing for the growth and development of young men.

THE PREVENTION OF INJURIES

Accidents in wrestling can be prevented by beginning the instruction with the wrestlers on the mat, instead of on their feet, and by teaching some of the blocking and countering maneuvers first. The early class periods are devoted primarily to maneuvers and activities that provide instruction and practice in rolling, falling, blocking, and recovering on the mat. The work progresses from pinning situations and the referee's position on the mat to the neutral position on the knees, to the rear standing position, and finally to the neutral standing position.

Drills to strengthen the neck and develop flexibility in the trunk and thorax are also introduced early in the course to prevent injuries to these parts. The blocks for the nelsons along with the escapes from the half nelson and reverse nelson pins are used for this purpose. As the students develop competence in executing these maneuvers, the resistance can be increased, thereby requiring a greater force on the part of both wrestlers in completing the movement. Such physical requirements as neck strength, trunk flexibility, over-all body strength, endurance, balance, leverage, and maneuverability are all developed by this practice. Whenever possible, the wrestling maneuvers instead of calisthenics are used in this manner to provide for the physical development as well as the development of the effective skills in competitive matches.

THE DEVELOPMENT OF A SOUND AND FAVORABLE ATTITUDE

Good mental condition as well as good physical condition is essential for effective performance in wrestling. The development of a favorable attitude toward the sport is dependent on gradual development of proficiency and prevention of embarrassing situations that result from a lack of skill and knowledge. Confidence is gained through progressive step-by-step learning. Insofar as possible, the introduction of each new maneuver is practiced until the student becomes proficient in the execution of it.

Competition involving the acquired skills is intended to motivate the students. Frequent scrimmages in maintaining and releasing the various holds, and in blocking and countering the maneuvers, provide experiences that interest the skilled wrestler as well as the beginner. Furthermore these scrimmages provide a meaningful experience in understanding the contribution that wrestling makes to the development of over-all body strength, physical fitness, and personal defense tactics. These outcomes are emphasized throughout the course, to induce a favorable attitude toward wrestling by creating a personal desire for maximum growth, development, and efficiency in the sport.

THE RAPID DEVELOPMENT OF COMPETENCE

Owing to the limited time provided for the course, the rapid development of competence is an important concern in arranging the teaching progression. Consideration has been given in the preceding discussion to factors that provide for efficiency in learning. A curriculum based on the characteristics, needs, interests, and objectives of the students is designed to accomplish the most effective learning in the least amount of time.

In addition to the qualities outlined in the preceding text, there are other basic physical capabilities such as balance, speed, leverage, and precision of movement, which need to be stressed early in the program in order to accelerate the development of competent wrestling performance. The warm-up activities and the preliminary maneuvers provide for the development of these basic physical requisites and they are emphasized throughout the course.

Another factor that contributes to the rapid development of competence is the arrangement of the holds and maneuvers into sequences for their presentations. A sequence is a chain of maneuvers that includes the set-up or preliminary action and follows through to a pinning hold in most cases. This arrangement prepares the student for the actual situation he is likely to encounter in a wrestling match.

Frequent scrimmages and contests against time are also factors in speeding up the learning process.

SUMMARY

By using the criteria of needs, objectives, safety, interests, and competence as bases, a teaching progression of wrestling maneuvers has been developed. There are numberless holds, maneuvers, countermaneuvers, and blocks that contribute to effective wrestling. But the drills and sequences that are given in this book have been found through experience to be the most effective in relation to the time available and the criteria set forth for this curriculum.

The next chapters of this book explain and illustrate in detail the prescribed maneuvers arranged in the teaching progression, commencing with the warm-up activities. Following this there is a summary which provides a list of the holds and maneuvers classified according to their function as a takedown, breakdown, ride, escape, reversal or pin. Chapter 6 of this book contains an outline of the content for each of the 30 lessons of the course. Samples of some of the materials for the course are reproduced in the Appendix.

2

Warm-up and Conditioning Individual and Dual Activities Performed in Mass Formation

I. MAT DRILL

The mat drill is a mass-exercise activity that involves the practice of individual wrestling techniques. This drill is similar to the so-called football grass drill, except that the action applies to skills in wrestling. The members of the class space themselves over the mat area so that there is at least a double-arm interval between them.

a. Start. The start is a standing position with the hands resting on the legs just above the knees. The arms are straight and the weight of the upper body is resting on the hands.

b. On Guard. By removing the hands from the legs, and keeping the inside of the upper arms pressed against the sides of the chest and taking a short step forward with either foot, the wrestler's "on guard" position is assumed.

FIRST SERIES.   The first series of moves involves four techniques: spot running, blocking a leg tackle, defensive referee's position, and standing up.

c. Spot Running.   Spot running is running in place, keeping the feet close to the mat in order to touch the feet on the mat as rapidly as possible. Whenever the wrestlers come to a standing position during any part of the "mat drill," they should be spot running.

d. Block.   On the command "block," the wrestlers drop their hands to the mat, extending their legs backward and spreading them out. The back is arched a little, with the stomach pressed toward the mat.

e. Position.   The wrestlers push back into a good base on their knees. This is known as the "defensive referee's position on the mat."

f. Up.   On the command "up," the wrestlers push back to a squat position and stand up by extending their legs.

g. Spot Run.   As the wrestlers reach the standing position, they start spot running immediately.

NOTE: All moves from (c) to (g) inclusive can be repeated several times.

SECOND SERIES.   The second series of moves involves a bucking movement from the hands and knees position.

h. Buck.   Start from position (e), the defensive referee's position on the mat. On the command "buck," the wrestlers keep their hands on the mat and drop their heads in between their arms as they extend their legs, making a steep slide out of their backs. As soon as the legs are extended, all the body weight should be on the feet, with the hands sliding back toward the legs as the wrestlers try to touch their elbows to the mat. This is the move-

ment a wrestler would use to back out from under an opponent who was riding too high on his back.

Down.   On the command "down," the wrestlers return to the starting position (e) on the hands and knees.

NOTE: This second series can be repeated and can also be worked in with the first series.

THIRD SERIES.   The third series provides the technique for recovering to a position on the knees from a prone position on the stomach.

i. Front.   On the command "front," the wrestlers drop to a prone position, lying on their stomachs with their arms bent and pulled in close to their sides and under their chests.

j. Right or Left.   On the command "right," they roll to a cuddle position on their right sides. On the command "left," they extend their legs, rolling

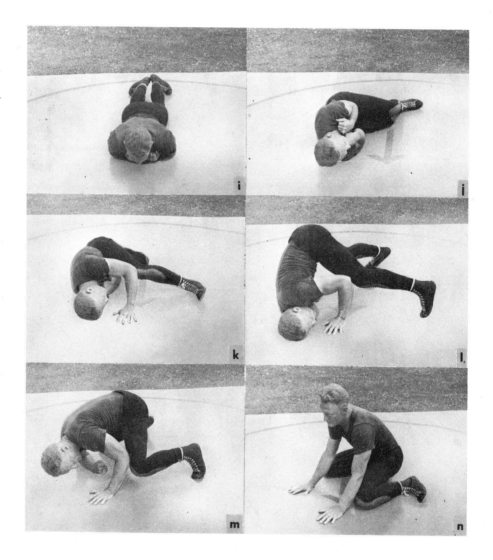

to their stomachs and into a cuddle position on their left sides. In the cuddle position the elbows are bent and held against the sides. The knees are bent and pulled up toward the chest with the top leg forward.

k. Hand on Mat. From a position on their right sides, the wrestlers place their left hands on the mat close to their faces and step their left feet forward toward their heads, placing the left feet on the mat close to their left hands.

l. Front Bridge. The wrestlers turn into a front bridge on their right shoulders by turning on their toes as they support themselves on their right shoulders and left hands. The feet are spread and the knees are wide apart.

m. Push Back. The knees are set out wide and lowered to the mat as the wrestlers push on the mat with their hands to raise their shoulders off the mat and move back to a position on their knees.

n. Recover. On the command "recover," the wrestlers push back into a position on their hands and knees, sitting on their legs with their toes turned out.

NOTE: As soon as they are competent in this series, the wrestlers will execute positions (k), (l), (m), and (n) in one continuous maneuver on the command "recover." From the position on the knees, the command "up" can be given, and this third series can be worked into the drill with the first two series.

FOURTH SERIES. The fourth series is called "Bridging Right and Left" and consists of bridging from the back to the right or left shoulder and recovering to a standing position.

o. Back. On the command "back," the wrestlers drop to a backward lying position on the mat, with their hands on their chests, feet on the mat, and the legs in position for a back bridge.

p. Right or Left. On the command "right," the wrestlers do a back bridge on their right shoulders, pulling their right elbows under their right sides and placing their left hands on the mat close to their faces.

q. Turn. On the command "turn," they turn into a front bridge on the right shoulders as in (l).

r. Recover.   On the command "recover," the wrestlers use both hands to push up from the mat into a standing position, spot running until the command "back" is given.

NOTE: The same procedure can be directed to the left and up. After competence is achieved in the execution of this exercise, the wrestlers should bridge, turn, and recover in a continuous maneuver in the direction of the command "right" or the command "left." It is best to alternate right and left and give enough time in spot running for them all to face forward and space themselves equidistant apart while they are spot running. Any of the first three series can be worked back into this drill from the spot-running position.

FIFTH SERIES

Sit-out and Turn-in.   The "sit-out and turn-in" is described and illustrated as a dual activity in paragraphs 3a, 3b, 3c and 3d which follow and in maneuver 4 of Chapter 3, page 19. It should first be practiced as an individual activity along with the other exercises in the preceding series. The action may consist of a series of sit-outs to the same side or alternated to "right" or "left," as in the bridging drill.

II. INDIVIDUAL EXERCISES AND DUAL ACTIVITIES

1. BRIDGING AND BACK PUSH-UPS

a. High Bridge.   From the "back" position (1a) the wrestlers push onto their heads and into a high bridge, trying to touch the nose and chin on the mat. It may be necessary for some to support this bridge by stretching their arms backward over their shoulders and placing their hands on the mat. After neck strength is developed, all wrestlers should be able to do high bridges with their arms folded in front of their chests.

b. Forward.   From the high bridge position the wrestlers rock forward until the back of the head supports the bridge. The back does not touch the mat in this position, and the wrestlers are ready to rock back into a high bridge. The exercise is repeated several times.

c. Back Push-up.   From the high bridge position the wrestlers place their hands on the mat under their shoulders and push up with the legs and arms into a high arch. The head is thrust backward under the back as the wrestler looks at the mat directly under him. On the command "down," the forehead is lowered to the mat, and the wrestlers are in position to repeat the exercise.

OTHER EXERCISES: Such activities as sit-ups, leg lifts, pull-ups, and push-ups can be practiced along with other exercises to develop flexibility **and** strengthen various parts of the body that may need development. **These**

special exercises are not included in this book because the emphasis here is on the development of wrestling techniques.

2. SPINNING. Spinning is an excellent conditioning activity and also contributes to the development of effective wrestling skills.

a. Start. One wrestler is on his hands and knees and the other is on top in a floating position.

b. Spin. The top wrestler spins to the right or left, keeping his chest in contact with the scapular area on the bottom man's back. The top man pivots on his chest and moves in a circular motion around the bottom man. He should travel 180 degrees on each move, completing the entire circle (360 degrees) in two moves. The wrestlers reverse positions every 20 or 30 seconds.

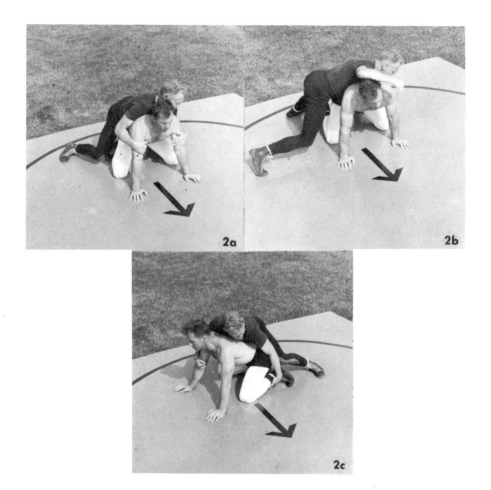

c. **Position.**   On the command "position," the top man quickly spins to the rear of the bottom man and attempts to break the bottom man down with one of the "breakdowns" explained in maneuver 11 of Chapter 3.   On the command "spin," the spinning is resumed.

NOTE: Another maneuver added later to the spinning drill is the "stand-up counter against the cross-face," after it is learned in maneuver 31 of Chapter 3.   On the command "cross-face," the top man spins to a cross-face position, and the bottom man counters with the stand-up as explained in maneuver 31.   On the command "spin," the wrestlers return to the mat, and the top man resumes his spinning.

3. SIT-OUT AND TURN-IN, TOP MAN FOLLOW

a. **Start.**   A is on the mat on his hands and knees, and B is on top in a floating position.

b. Sit. A sits out to a position on his left side, as described in maneuver 4 of Chapter 3; B follows in a floating position on top, moving on his feet and holding onto A's arms.

c. Turn. A turns into a front bridge, and B maintains the floating position on top.

d. Recover. A sets his knees wide and recovers into a position on his hands and knees as B follows in the floating position on top.

4. DUAL BRIDGING (REVERSALS FROM ARM LOCK AND BODY LOCK PIN)

a. Start. B is in a back bridge position and A is on top on the right side of B, with his chest on B's chest. Each has a body lock with the right arm while the left arm of each is used to hold the opponent's right arm and lock it into the side.

b. Bridge and Over. B executes a high bridge to the left onto his left shoulder, turning A with him until A's back is toward the mat. A places his head on the mat as he goes over and prepares to land in a back bridging position as B turns into the top position.

c. Bridge and Over. From the back bridging position with B on top, A follows through to a high bridge on his left shoulder, turning B with him. As B goes over, he turns on his head and prepares to land in a bridging position.

d. Bridge and Continue. B lands in a bridging position with A on top, as at the start (a). The bridge-overs, (b) and (c), are repeated three or four times before stopping.

3

Wrestling Maneuvers in a Teaching Progression

Throughout the thirty-eight sequences that follow, A performs the essential action against B's resistance. In the accompanying illustrations A is dressed in the black uniform and B in the white tights.

1. BLOCK FOR QUARTER NELSON

a. START: QUARTER NELSON POSITION. A is on his hands and knees in the defensive referee's position. B is on his knees to the left of A, opposite A's left shoulder. B's left hand is hooked over A's head, with his right arm under A's left arm and his right hand hooked over his own left wrist. B pulls down and in on A's head. B increases the leverage by forcing his right elbow up and into A's left side.

b. LOCK ARM. A locks his left arm around B's right arm above the elbow, pulling the arm down into his groin. At the same time A raises his head backward and looks over his right shoulder. This causes B's hand to slip down the head to the neck, thus reducing the leverage applied by B.

c. LUNGE. A keeps B's left arm locked as he lunges in a circular motion. This movement carries him down to his left side, pulling B down with him and knocking B off balance by a thrust of his left hip against B. To accomplish this, A pushes against the mat with his right foot and right hand and rolls to his left side as he drives his left hip into B's right side and rotates his upper body away from B. A should be cautioned against exerting excessive force because of the danger of injury to B's shoulder. Only half-resistance should be offered by B, with A applying just enough force to bring B to the mat. B protects himself by releasing the grip and pulling his right arm under him as he places his hand on the mat.

d. FOLLOW-THROUGH. A follows the action in (c) by bringing B down to a prone position on the mat.

2. BLOCK FOR THREE-QUARTER NELSON

a. START: THREE-QUARTER NELSON POSITION. A is on his hands and knees in the referee's position on the mat. B is on his knees, with his right knee between A's legs. B's left hand is hooked over A's head, and his right arm reaches under A's chest to the far side of A's head, where his right hand hooks over his left hand. B's right shoulder is under the near side of A's chest. B pulls down and in on A's head, pushing his right shoulder up against A's chest to increase the leverage.

b. BLOCK. A reaches his left hand across the mat under his right side

to lock B's arm as he drops his left shoulder toward the mat and thrusts his left hip into B's right side.

c. DRIVE.   As A thrusts his left hip into B's side, he pushes against the mat with his right foot, rotating his upper body away from B and dropping to the mat on his left shoulder, if necessary, to release the hold.

Both wrestlers should observe the caution described in maneuver 1(c) in regard to limiting the applied force and resistance to about half-strength so as to prevent injury to B's right shoulder.

NOTE: The blocking action for the quarter and the three-quarter nelsons can be used as an exercise to strengthen the neck as well as to develop protective skill against the nelsons.

This action consists of two parts:

1. B forces A's head down and in.
2. A forces his head back up and away.

These movements are repeated as B retains the lock on A's head. The force and resistance exerted by each wrestler should be balanced to permit the full extent of the movements without breaking the hold. The force is increased as the neck gets stronger.

The complete exercise consists of five or six repetitions of the action from each side and for each type of nelson.

3. KNEE RECOVERY FROM A PRONE POSITION

a. START. A is on his stomach in a "clam-up position." His arms are bent and tucked under his chest. B is in a sprawl position on a diagonal to A and is driving with his legs to force his weight against A's left buttock.

b. CUDDLE LEFT. A cuddles on his left side to keep B in back of him by pulling both knees up toward his chest and stepping his right foot forward.

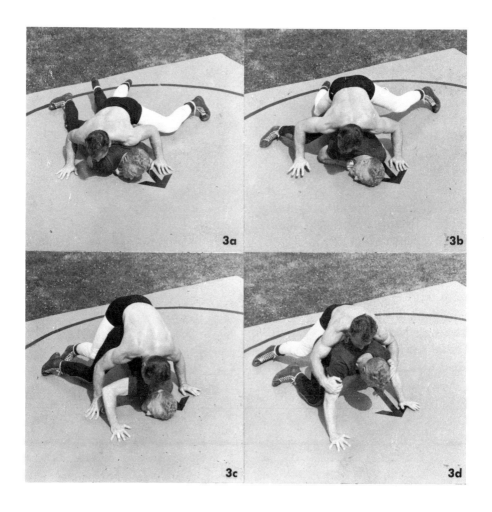

c. FRONT BRIDGE. A turns into a front bridge on his left shoulder and sets his knees wide, ready to place them on the mat.

d. RECOVER. A sets his knees wide on the mat as he pushes up with his hands to a wide base on his hands and knees.

NOTE: Do the same exercise to the opposite side, starting with "Cuddle Right." Alternate right and left for five or six repetitions.

4. SIT-OUT AND TURN-IN TO CRAWFISH

a. START. The start is in the referee's position with A underneath and B on top. B's right arm is around A's waist.

b. STEP AND REACH. A steps up and out on his right foot and moves his left arm forward on the mat to move his ankle and arm away from B.

c. SIT. A swings his left leg under his right, bringing his left elbow into his stomach. As he lands on the mat on his left side, A raises his right leg

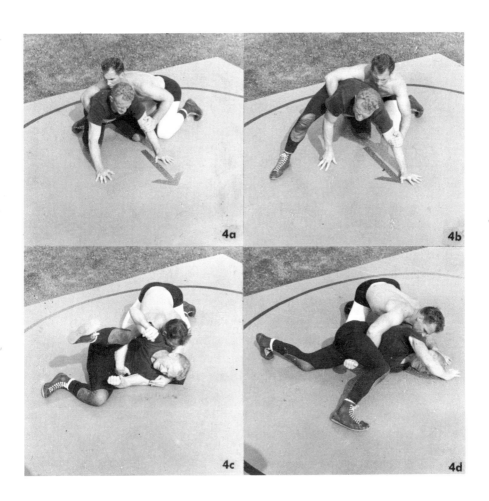

forward and moves his left leg backward in a scissors position, keeping his knees bent and his legs wide apart.

d. TURN.   Continuing the scissors action of his legs, A places his feet on the mat to turn into a front bridge on his left shoulder. A places his right hand on the mat in front of his forehead. A's left arm is straightening out under his body for the rotation outward on the recovery.

e. FRONT BRIDGE.   A pivots on his left shoulder and balls of both feet into a front bridge on his left shoulder. His left arm continues to rotate outward, and his right hand is placed on the mat for balance. Both knees are set out wide for the recovery.

f. RECOVER.   A sets his right knee on the mat and rotates his left arm out and around B's back to start the crawfish maneuver.

g. CRAWFISH.   A bucks into a position on his feet, pivoting on his right hand with his left arm hooked deep around B's ribs. B's right arm has started to slide off A's back as A keeps his head down to allow for this action.

h. STEP-OVER.   A continues the pivot on his right hand as he steps his left leg over to the far side of B and pulls B under him with his left arm. A extends his left hand into B's crotch for the inside crotch-pry leverage and drives off on his left foot to apply pressure against B's left hip with the inside of his left thigh. A's right hand remains on the mat until he maintains stability on top of B or breaks him down.

5. ESCAPE FROM HALF NELSON AND CROTCH PIN

a. START.   B, on top, has a deep half nelson with his right arm and a

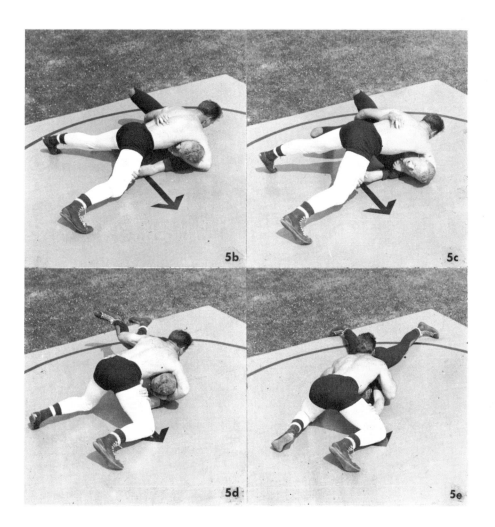

crotch hold with his left. He maintains good balance in a chest-on-chest position. His legs are extended, with knees slightly bent and toes turned out. The weight is on the balls of feet and chest. A is underneath on his back and turned on his left side.

b. CUDDLE POSITION. A turns to his left side. As he pushes B's right leg away with his left hand, he reaches his right hand under B's chest as far as possible and around the back of B, getting his right shoulder under B's chest. A tries to work his left knee under B as he pushes B down toward his legs.

NOTE: A is somewhat relaxed on his left side and his legs are in position to bridge.

c. BRIDGE. A bridges on his left shoulder and head. He pushes on B's left leg and tries to turn B over by lifting with his right arm around B's

back. B maintains his balance in a toe-chest position by moving his center of gravity over A's left arm and moving his right leg out to brace against B's force.

d. DROP AND PIVOT ON LEFT HIP. A drops to his left hip and extends his legs, swinging his left leg under his right as he pushes B away with his hands on B's thighs.

e. EXTEND LEGS AND SPIN TO STOMACH. A spins to prone position on stomach, with legs and arms extended and hands on B's thighs just above the knees, pushing B away to keep him from spinning behind.

f. PUSH-UP. A pulls his arms back and quickly pushes up to a position on his hands and knees, keeping the back of his head up tight against the chest of B.

g. SPIN AND CRAWFISH. As B attempts to spin behind, A throws his right arm around B's back and bucks into a crawfish position. As A drives off of his left foot and left hand, he raises his right leg to step over B's legs and pulls B under him.

h. STEP-ACROSS AND DRIVE. As A pulls B under him to the mat, he steps his right leg across to the far side of B and drives B into the mat with the leverage from the inside of his thigh against B's hip and his shoulder in B's back.

6. ESCAPE FROM REVERSE NELSON AND CROTCH PIN

a. START. B, on top, has a deep reverse nelson with his left arm and a crotch hold with his right. He maintains good balance in a toe-chest position. A is underneath on his back. He tries to turn to his right side.

b. CUDDLE. A turns to his right side. As he pushes B's left leg away with his right hand, he reaches his left hand under B's chest as far as possible and

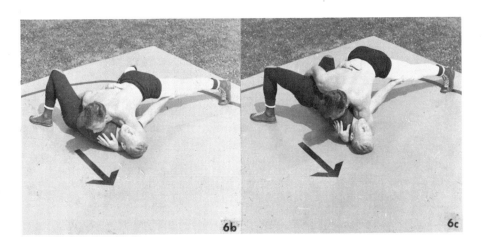

around the back of B, getting his left shoulder under B's chest. A tries to work his right knee under B as he pushes B down toward his legs.

c. BRIDGE ON RIGHT SHOULDER. A bridges on his right shoulder and head. He pushes on B's left leg and tries to turn B over by lifting with his left arm around B's back. B maintains his balance in toe-chest position by moving his center of gravity over A's right arm and moving his left leg out to brace against B's force.

d. DROP AND TURN. A places his right hand against his stomach, drops his hips to the mat, and rolls to his left side, pulling his left arm out and forcing his right arm through as far as possible. B keeps his chest tight against A and maneuvers to keep his center of gravity balanced on A.

e. BRIDGE ON LEFT SHOULDER. As A bridges on his left shoulder, he pushes against B's chin with his left hand and forces his right arm out from under B as far as possible.

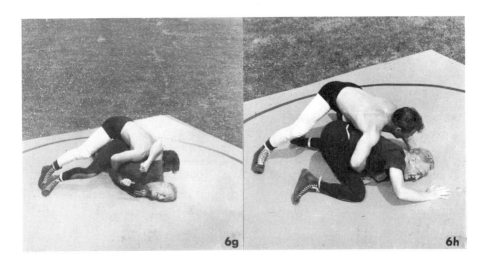

f. DROP AND SHOOT ARM.   A drops his hips to mat, shoots his right arm free from under B, and turns on his left side away from B.

g. FORCE HEAD AND TURN.   A uses the back of his upper right arm to force B's head down and then turns into a front bridge on his left shoulder to recover.

h. RECOVER.   As A turns into a front bridge * on his left shoulder, he sets his knees wide and recovers to a position on his hands and knees, with B following on top.

7. RELEASE TIGHT WAIST

a. START.   A is on his left side on the mat with B's right arm wrapped deep around his waist.   A is held close to B by the leverage in B's right arm. B pushes his shoulder into A's ribs and pulls down on A's left hip with his right hand.

b. PULL ELBOW AND BRIDGE.   A takes a good hold on B's right arm with both hands and pulls B's elbow into A's chest as he bridges into a back bridge on his left shoulder.

c. TURN INTO FRONT BRIDGE.   A turns into a front bridge on his left shoulder as he maintains the pull on B's elbow.

d. RECOVER.   A sets his knees wide and recovers to a position on his hands and knees as he releases B's arm.   B floats into the top position as A recovers.

* The front bridge is learned in basic drills used for warm-up (see Chapter 2, Third Series, (k-n).

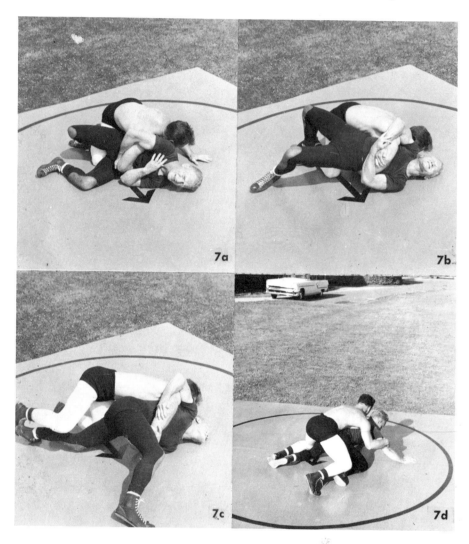

NOTE: It may be necessary for A to extend his left leg under B and roll to his stomach in order to get his right knee on the mat for the recovery.

8. RELEASE FOR BAR ARM AND OUTSIDE CROTCH

a. START: BAR ARM AND OUTSIDE CROTCH POSITION. A is on his left side on the mat in a cuddle position. B slides his left hand down through the crook in A's left elbow and underhooks A's left forearm as deep as possible, keeping the thumb alongside the fingers under A's forearm. B applies leverage by keeping his left arm straight and prying upward on A's left forearm as he leans his arm across A's back, pressing his left shoulder into the area at the top of A's right scapula. B's right hand is hooked over

A's right buttock. His right knee is against A's left wrist and his left knee is drawn up close to A's left shoulder. B's toes on both feet are turned outward.

b. BUCK. A gathers his legs in under him and keeps his lower back pushed into B. By a quick buck upward, B is raised enough to permit A to turn toward his stomach and rotate his arm, extending it outward and ahead from under B. The left leg is extended in this position. If B is exerting a great deal of force to maintain the bar arm, it will also be necessary to extend the right leg and go into a prone position on the stomach in order to release the arm.

c. TURN AND RELEASE ARM. A turns toward his stomach, supporting his weight on his toes and the front of his left shoulder and chest, as he throws his left arm outward and ahead, turning the palm downward to stretch his arm away from the grasp of his opponent. A continues the forward movement of his hand, pulling his left arm into his side and placing his hand on the mat under his left shoulder in a position to push up and back for the recovery. All of this must be done quickly to prevent B from getting a half nelson when the arm is moving out and ahead.

d. RECOVERY. A sets his knees wide and uses both hands to push up from the mat and back to a position on his knees as B recovers to a control position on top.

NOTE: It may be necessary for A to extend both his legs and roll to his stomach to release his wrist. In this case he would recover by a quick push-up with his arms, pulling his legs under him in a wide-spread position.

9. BLOCKING NEAR-SIDE HALF NELSON WITH ELBOW-LOCK ROLL TO A KEY LOCK

a. START. The start is in the referee's position with A underneath and B on top. B's right arm is around A's waist and his left hand is on A's left elbow. B reaches under A's left arm with his left arm and places his left hand on the back of A's head for a half nelson.

b. RAISE UP AND REACH OVER ARM. A raises his upper body and turns to the left, reaching his left arm high around B's left upper arm.

c. LOCK ARM. A pulls down and in on B's left arm to lock it into his side as he raises his head and turns it away from B. This causes B's hand to slip from the head to the neck of A.

d. LUNGE. A keeps B's left arm locked as he rotates his upper body away from B and down to the mat on his left shoulder, pulling B down with him and knocking B off balance by a thrust of his left hip against B.

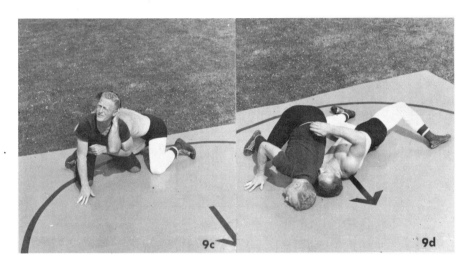

e. SPIN ACROSS.   A maintains the lock on B's arm and pivots on his left shoulder and right hand to swing his left leg over B, following with his right leg.

f. TAKE HOLD OF WRIST.   As A completes the spin across B, he keeps B's arm locked under his left arm and takes hold of B's left wrist with his right hand to bring it down under B's back.

g. SET THE WRIST.   A moves B's left hand under B's left side and locks B's arm in this position by holding B's wrist with both hands.

h. KEY LOCK.   A removes his hands from B's wrist and slides his right arm under B's elbow, hooking his right hand on his upper left arm and his left hand on his upper right arm, to fold his arms around B's arm.   A flexes both his arms, pulling them in close to B to make B's elbow stick out.

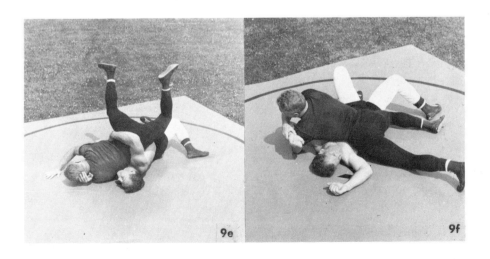

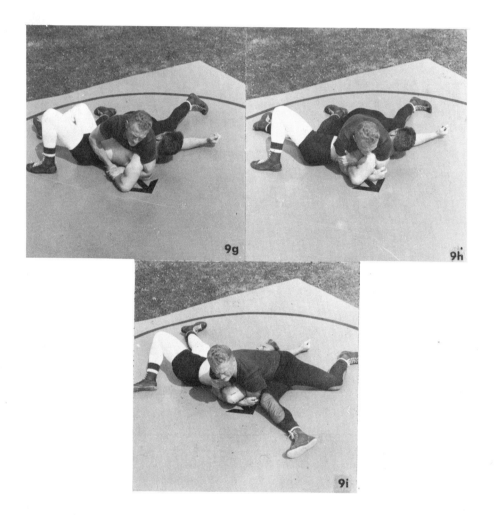

i. PINNING POSITION. A moves around B's head to a sitting position on his right hip with his legs in a running stride, with his right leg forward, and with his back pressed against B's head. If B gives any resistance, A can squeeze harder on the arm and press his ribs down on B's shoulder to immobilize him.

10. DOUBLE ARM LOCK AND ROLL

a. START. A is on his hands and knees. B's chest is on A's head, with right arm hooked under A's left arm. B's left arm is extended over A's right shoulder into A's crotch. In this position B can hold off A and prevent A from getting hold of B's legs.

b. MOVE IN, HEAD UP. A moves in on his hands and knees, raising his

head up under B's right arm and locking his right arm around B's left arm above the elbow.

c. LOCK ARMS AND SIT THROUGH.   A keeps B's arm locked with his right arm and takes hold of B's right arm with his left hand on the triceps, pulling B's arm down onto his shoulder.   A sets his right leg under his left, pulling B in under him as he maintains the lock on both of B's arms.

d. BALANCE.   A maintains the locks on B's arms.   He keeps his balance by pushing his back against B's chest when B is bridging left.   When B

bridges to his right, A lowers his center of gravity and extends his weight away from B.

e. RECOVER.   If A loses the locks on B's arms, A turns on his right shoulder to a chest-on-chest position on B, taking an inside crotch hold with his left hand and a nelson with his right.

f. CONTROL.   A maintains control with the crotch hold and half nelson in the chest-on-chest position.

11. BREAKDOWNS FOR THE SPINNING DRILL

INTRODUCTION.   Three breakdowns are introduced to be used in the spinning drill. (Chapter 2, II, 2a, 2b, 2c.) On the command "position,"

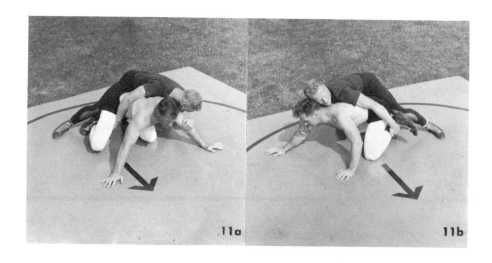

given during the spinning exercise, the top man attempts to unbalance the bottom man by removing a part of his base and forcing him in the direction of the unstable part of his base. The bottom man resists this action, trying to maintain a stable position on his hands and knees.

These breakdowns should be learned from both sides, and one or all may be tried during each "position" interval until the signal is given to resume the spinning.

   a. INSIDE CROTCH PRY AND NEAR-ARM PULL. A's right hand with palm turned out is placed against the inside of B's right thigh. A's right leg is behind and forcing against B's right buttock. A's left hand is hooked on the crook of B's left elbow. A pulls back and in on B's left arm, trying to force it into B's left side. A, using his right arm as a lever, leans diagonally forward across B's back to pry up on the inside of B's right thigh as he pushes against B's right buttock with his leg to force B in the direction of his left arm, trying to break him down to his side on the mat. B tries to maintain his stability by lowering his chest toward the mat as he pulls away from the direction of force and widens his base.

   b. FAR-ANKLE AND NEAR-ARM PULL. The action is similar to that for the crotch pry. A has his left hand hooked on B's left ankle and is pulling on it instead of prying into the crotch to unbalance B in the direction of B's right arm, which is being pulled in. This action takes place on the side opposite to that of the preceding action for the crotch pry.

   c. TIGHT WAIST AND NEAR-ARM PULL. The action is similar to that for the crotch pry. A has his arm locked deep around B's waist instead of applying the leverage in the crotch.

NOTE: In each of these breakdowns it may not be possible to pull B's arm back against his side. However, if the pulling force is maintained on B's arm, it will set B's arm, i.e., preventing him from moving it out on the mat to widen his base. The force exerted by A's other arm, along with that of the leg behind B, can then be used to drive B over and beyond the "set" arm on the mat, thus breaking him down.

12. KNEE TAP AS COUNTER FOR DOUBLE UNDERHOOKS

a. START. A and B are on their knees and B is holding A away from his legs by locking both his arms under A's arms near the shoulders and hooking his hands on A's back. A has his head under B's right arm pit and is pushing in that direction.

b. BLOCK THE KNEE AND LOCK THE ARM. A moves his right knee in closer to B as he reaches his right hand diagonally across the mat, placing it on the outside of B's right knee. At the same time, A takes hold of B's right arm at the triceps, locking B's arm with his left arm. He then steps back onto his left foot, raising his left knee off the mat.

c. BREAKDOWN. A brings B to the mat by bracing his right hand against the outside of B's right knee and pulling B forward and downward. B is rotated onto his back as A follows through with an upward pull on B's right arm, which remains locked under A's left arm. A places his right hand against B's left hip and pushes B away in order to get his head out from under B's right arm pit. B's right arm remains locked under A's left arm, and A supports his left arm against his left thigh.

d. CONTROL. After A gets his head out, he steps his left foot closer to B, extending B's right arm and keeping B's right arm locked under his left

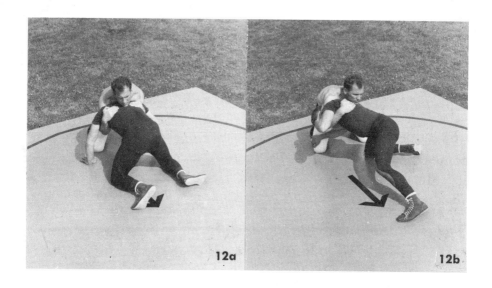

12a   12b

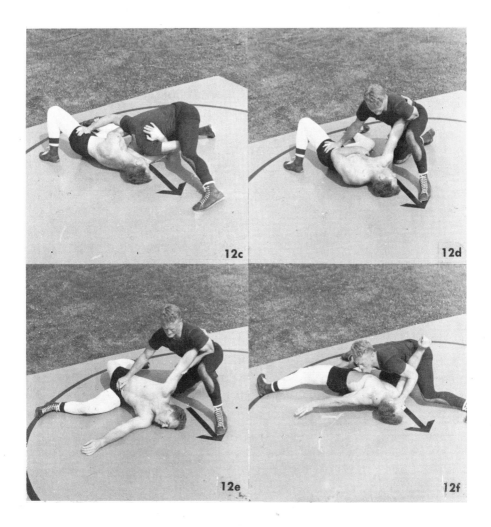

arm which is supported on his left thigh. A continues to push on B's left hip with his right hand, to keep B in position on his back.

e. ROLL AWAY FROM A.   As B rolls away, A pulls on B's locked arm to keep B under control.

f. ROLL TOWARD A.   When B rolls toward A, A moves into a reverse nelson and crotch hold for a pinning position.

13. FAR-SIDE ROLL TO REVERSE NELSON AND CRADLE

a. START.   The start is in the referee's position with A underneath and B on top.   B's right arm is around A's waist.

b. SIT ON HEEL.   A takes hold of B's right wrist with his right hand, turns

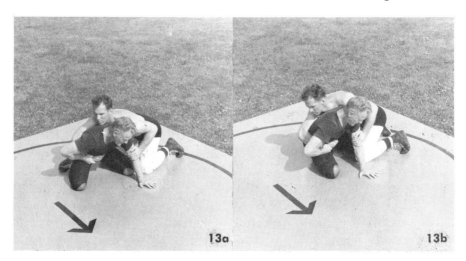

his right foot in, and sits on his right heel as he moves his legs under B as far as possible.

c. ROLL.   A keeps B's right arm tight around his waist. As A rolls to his right hip and right elbow, he hooks his left instep under B's right knee and hooks his left hand on the outside of B's upper left leg.

d. KICK OVER.   A adds to the momentum of the roll by using his left instep to thrust B's right leg up and over, keeping hold of B's wrist and leg with his right and left hands, respectively.

e. RIGHT ANGLE AND SCISSORS LEGS.   A swings his legs at a right angle to B, moving his left leg under and behind his right leg, ready to turn on his toes into a position on his knees. He retains the hold on B's wrist with his right hand but releases the hold on B's leg, placing his left hand on the mat on the left side of B.

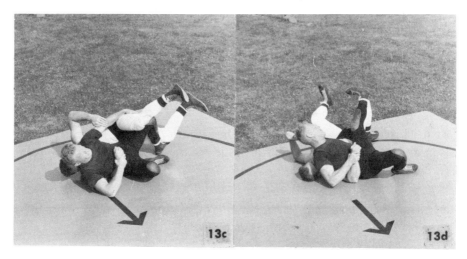

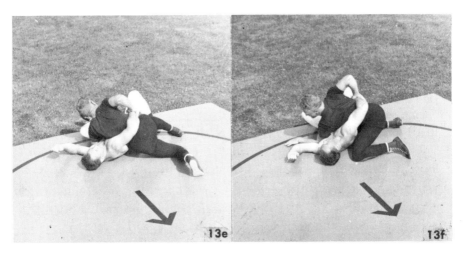

f. RECOVER ON KNEES.   A turns on his toes as in a front bridge and recovers to his knees, pushing his knees against B's back. A's left hand is on
the mat for balance. He continues to hold B's wrist with his right hand and
pulls B's right arm tightly around his back.

g. REVERSE NELSON AND INSIDE CROTCH.   A underhooks B's head with
his left arm as he releases B's left wrist and gets an inside crotch hold with
his right arm, with his forearm under B's left leg.

h. CRADLE.   A raises B's left leg with his right arm to lock his hands by
hooking the fingers of one hand into the hooked fingers of the other. By
extending his left leg and pressing his hip to the mat and against B's left
arm, A can wedge B into a tight pinning situation. A should keep his arms
flexed and his elbows pulled in close to his body for the maximum leverage,
putting a twist on B's neck as it is pinched in the crook of A's left elbow.

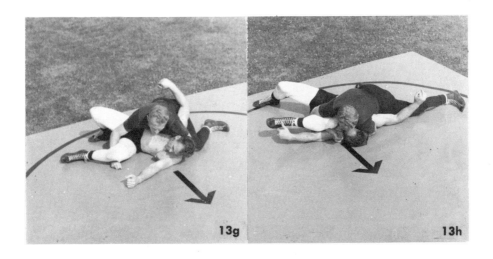

14. INSIDE CROTCH PRY AND ARM PULL TO BAR ARM AND HALF NELSON HOLDS

a. START. The start is in the referee's position with B underneath and A on top. A's right arm is around B's waist.

b. PIVOT BEHIND. A drops his right hand into B's crotch, with the palm of his hand against the inside of B's right thigh. At the same time A steps onto his right foot, behind B, forcing against B's right buttock with the inside of his right thigh. A keeps his left hand hooked on the crook of B's left elbow and his left knee remains on the mat outside of B's left ankle.

c. LEVERAGE. A leans diagonally forward across B's back, and uses his right arm as a lever across B's side. Pushing against B's right buttock with the inside of his right thigh, he forces B off balance to the left. At the same

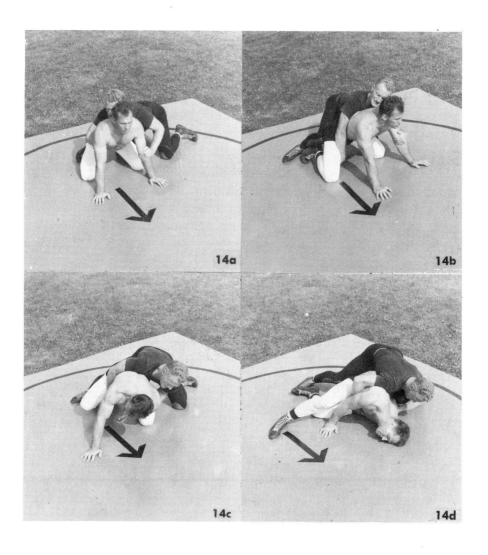

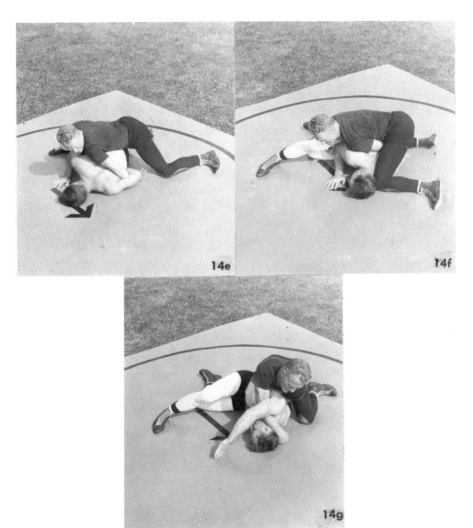

time he pulls B's left arm into his side to remove B's support in the direction of the force.

d. BREAKDOWN. As B falls to the mat, A jerks B's left elbow out to the side to prevent B from catching A in a roll. A takes hold of the fingers of B's left hand with his right hand to keep B's left arm set in that position.

e. BAR ARM. As A maintains the hold on B's fingers with his right hand, he reaches through the crook of B's left elbow with his left hand, underhooking B's upper forearm as far as possible. A applies leverage by extending his left arm across B's upper back and leaning his left shoulder into B's back.

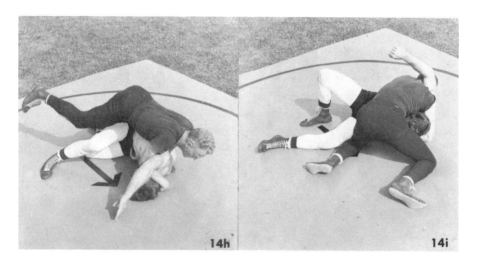

f. BAR ARM AND OUTSIDE CROTCH POSITION.   As A moves his left knee into B's neck and his right knee into B's wrist against the lower part of B's back, he releases the fingers of the right hand and takes an outside crotch hold on B's right leg, keeping the leverage across B's upper back with his left arm.

g. HALF NELSON AND SET HEAD.   As B pushes on the mat with his right hand, A reaches his right arm under B's right arm and drops his fist to the mat across the back of B's head to set the head in a half nelson.   A keeps his right arm as straight as possible and retains the bar with his left arm on B's left arm.

h. SPIN ACROSS.   A steps over B, pivoting on his own right arm and chest

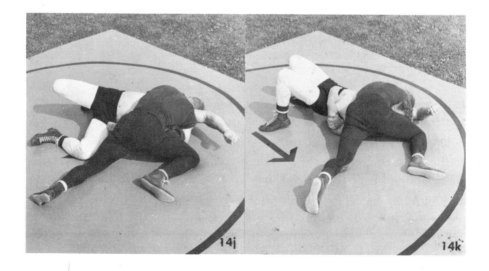

to get in front of B for a deep half nelson. A maintains the bar on B's left arm.

i. DEEP HALF NELSON. A places his right knee against B's head and his left knee into B's stomach as he moves his right arm as far as he can reach around B's neck. A retains the bar on B's left arm. A lifts B's head into the angle between his hip and stomach on his right side as he prepares to turn B onto his shoulder blades for the pinning position.

j. PRESS INTO PIN. A turns B onto his back by pressing against B's upper right arm with his neck pivoting B on B's left shoulder, keeping B's head twisted into his side. A moves his right knee in front of B's head and lowers his weight across B's lower chest by extending his left leg straight back away from B.

k. TWIST HEAD. A wedges B's head into a tight twist by holding it close to his side and moving his right thigh in under it for support. A's left leg is extended at right angles to B as A rolls his left side into B, centering his weight across the lower part of B's chest. A retains the bar on B's left arm.

15. COUNTER SIT-OUT AND TURN-IN WITH OVER DRAG

a. START. A is in the referee's position on top of B with his right arm around B's waist.

b. SIT-OUT. As B sits out, A is on his knees, and his right arm stays in contact with B's waist.

c. STEP-UP. As B turns into a front bridge to recover a neutral position, A loses the waist hold on B but maintains contact by moving his right hand

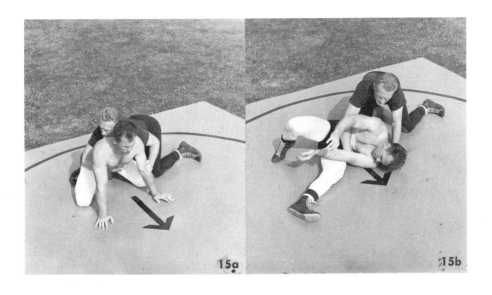

into B's right armpit from above. A steps up on his left foot to get in position for this action.

d. **HOOK ARM.**   A hooks his right hand into B's right armpit from above
as he prepares to jerk B forward and step behind him.

e. **PULL.**   A steps up to both feet and pulls with his right hand to turn B
in order to go behind him.

f. **GO BEHIND.**   A pivots behind B to a floating position on top by stepping forward with his right foot and swinging his left leg across B's legs to
brace his left foot on the mat at the left side of B.

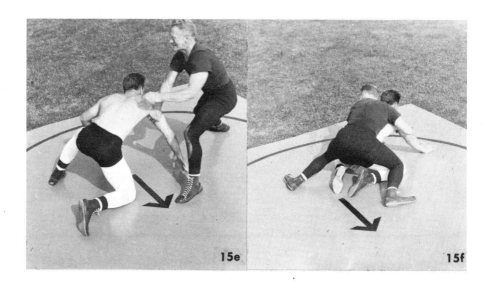

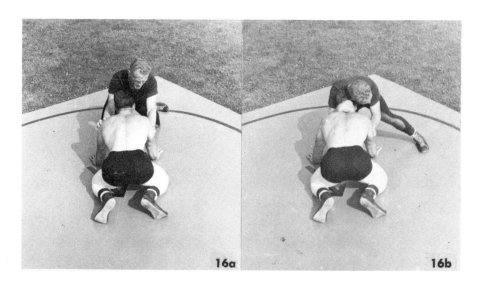

16. SNAPDOWN AND SPIN BEHIND

a. START.   A and B are on their knees facing each other, and A is pushing with both hands against B's shoulders.

b. MOVE IN AND PUSH.   A moves in and steps up on his left foot as he hooks his right hand on B's neck, maintaining the pushing action against B with his right forearm under B's chest and his left hand on B's right shoulder. B resists this action with enough forward force to keep from being pushed backward.

c. PULL.   When B forces forward, A changes from a push to a hard pull

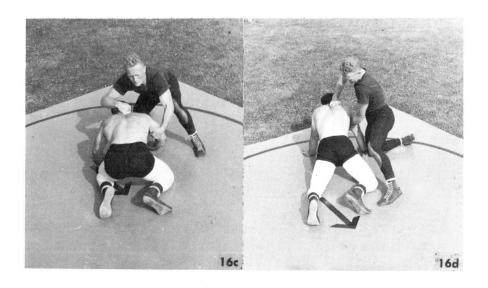

on B's neck with his right hand and overhooks B's right arm with his left hand to pull B forward as A steps to his feet to go behind.

d. SNAP DOWN. A jerks B forward with both hands and follows through, using his right hand to push B's head away and his left hand to push B's right arm aside as he moves to go behind B.

e. SPIN. With B off balance as a result of the snapdown, A drops into a spinning position on B's back, using his weight to increase B's instability as he moves behind B.

f. CONTROL. A spins in behind B into a floating position on top as B pushes back to recover from the snapdown.

17. SIT-OUT AND TURN-OUT

a. START. B is in the referee's position on top of A with his right arm around A's waist. A moves his right foot to the side.

b. SIT. A supports his weight on his right heel and left hand to swing his left leg forward, moving into a sitting position on his right buttock. At the same time A drives his right elbow toward his groin, keeping his forearm parallel to and inside his right thigh to lock B's right arm around his waist. A's left arm is pulled into his side to prevent B reaching under it. A is bending forward, and his heels are dug into the mat for support.

c. BRIDGE. A keeps B's arm locked under his right arm as he braces the back of his neck against B's right shoulder and executes a strong bridge. A supports much of his weight on B's right shoulder by keeping his head well back and raising his chest and hips up while he swings his buttocks toward his heels and moves his body straight ahead.

17a
17b
17c
17d
17e
17f

d. BREAKDOWN.   As A moves his body ahead, B's right arm is pulled forward and down to the mat under A.   A continues to move ahead, dropping his right knee outward until his right side touches the mat.

e. TURN.   A pivots immediately on his right foot, swinging his left leg over as he rolls off B's arm and away from him.

f. RECOVER.   A pushes back to a position on his hands and knees, facing B as B also recovers.

18. SWITCH TO TWO-ON-ONE BAR ARM

a. START.   B is in referee's position on top of A with his right arm around A's waist.

18b

18c

18d

18e

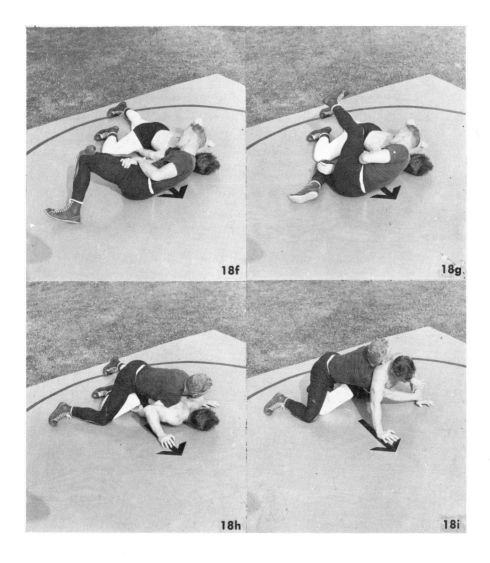

b. MOVE HAND.   A moves his left hand across his right hand and away from B.

c. HAND IN POCKET.   A extends his right leg backward and places his right hand on his right buttock as if reaching into his hip pocket.

d. SIT.   A swings his left leg under his right, pivoting on his left hand and right foot to a sitting position on the mat, with his right arm extended into B's crotch. A's right hand is pressed against the inside of B's right thigh, and he pulls on B's right arm with his left hand to get his armpit as close to B's armpit as possible.

e. EXTEND.   A extends his right arm and extends his body as he raises his buttocks off the mat and swings away from B. This forces B's right shoulder to the mat.

f. BREAKDOWN. A follows through with leverage on B's right arm until B is broken down on the mat. A may need to push B's right arm into A's crotch to avoid hurting it on the turn as B reacts automatically to remove his arm.

g. TURN. A swings his left leg upward and forward across B's thigh as he turns off his right elbow and right foot to the top position.

h. RECOVER. A steps across B with his left leg, and keeping his knees wide, he presses his weight into B by driving with his feet on the mat and forcing his abdomen against B's right hip.

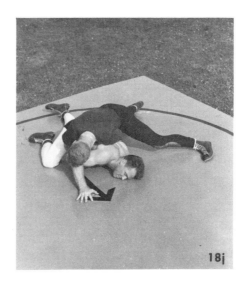

i. TWO-ON-ONE. As B tries to recover to his knees, A hooks both hands on B's left wrist, ready to pull B's arm in under him with his right hand as he applies the bar-arm leverage with his left arm.

j. LEVERAGE AND POSITION. A moves around to B's back, applying the leverage across B's upper back with his left arm as he holds B's wrist with his right hand. A keeps his legs spread and drives with his feet on the mat, forcing his left shoulder into B's right shoulder blade.

19. TWO-ON-ONE BAR ARM RIDE AND RELEASE FOR IT

a. START. A is on the mat in a cuddle position on his left side. B is on top with his right arm around A's waist and with his right hand gripping A's left wrist. B slides his left hand down through the crook in A's left elbow and underhooks A's left forearm as deep as possible, keeping his palm up and his thumb alongside his fingers under A's forearm. B is in a position

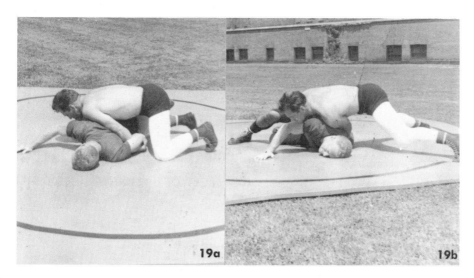

at right angles to A's back. B's left arm is straight, and his left shoulder is pressed into the area at the top of A's right scapula as he pries upward on A's right forearm.

b. LEVERAGE.   B stiffens his left arm, leaning into A with his left shoulder and bearing down with as much weight as possible on A's right shoulder blade. As he pries upward with his left hand under A's forearm, B maintains the grip with his right hand on A's left wrist. B's legs are well spread, and he drives forward from the balls of his feet in a circular motion around A's head.

c. RELEASE WRIST.   A draws up his right knee and braces his right foot on

the mat to push his hips backward against B. A uses his right hand to grip B's right wrist. By forcing down on B's wrist and driving off on his right foot to push B backward, A sets B's right arm down and away from his waist in an extended position. With B's right arm extended and held away from his body, A rotates his left wrist upward and over B's thumb, to release the grip B has with his right hand on A's wrist.

d. BUCK.   As A pushes B's right arm away, he gives a quick buck upward, turning into a front bridge on his left shoulder and rotating his left arm outward to stretch it away from B's left hand.

e. TURN.   A sets his knees wide and braces his right hand on the mat as he rotates his left arm away from B. From this position A must quickly turn his palm down and pull his left arm into his side, placing his left hand on the mat under his left shoulder in a position to push up and back for the recovery.

f. RECOVER.   A uses both hands to push up from the mat and back to a position on his knees as B recovers to a control position on top.

20. SWITCH SEQUENCE

B performs a series of switches and a roll as A blocks and counters to remain on top throughout the sequence of maneuvers.

a. START.   A is in the referee's position on top of B and has his right arm around B's waist.

b. ATTEMPT SWITCH AND BLOCK.   B attempts a right-handed switch, and A blocks with a deep waist hold. A raises his knees off the mat and drives

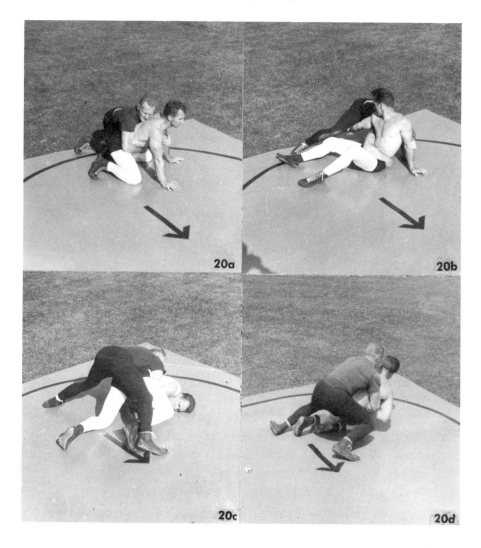

forward on his feet, forcing his right shoulder into B's right arm pit. A uses his right arm as a lever by forcing down on B's left hip with his right hand while pushing with his shoulder. By increasing this leverage and pulling in on B's left arm, B is forced down on his left side and shoulder.

c. TURN IN AND RECOVER. B swings his left leg under his right leg and pivots on the balls of his feet into a front bridge on his left shoulder, setting his knees out wide to recover on them. A steps across B's legs with his right leg and follows into a floating position on top of B with his right arm around B's waist.

d. SIDE ROLL. B takes hold of A's wrist with his right hand and moves his right leg toward his left leg to roll to his right hip and elbow for a far

side roll. A takes hold of B's right wrist with his left hand and moves in close to go along with the roll.

e. ROLL. A pulls B in snugly to his abdomen, keeping his knees wide as he is rolled to his right side by the force of B's roll.

f. ROLL THROUGH. Using the momentum created by B's force, A continues the roll, pulling B to the left and drawing his right instep under the crook of B's right knee to give B's right leg a thrust as he rolls B to the left.

g. RECOVER. A swings his left leg under his right and turns on the balls of his feet to set his knees out wide. As A recovers to his knees, his right arm remains around B's waist and B sits into a right-handed switch.

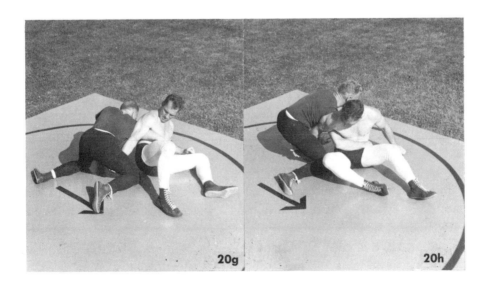

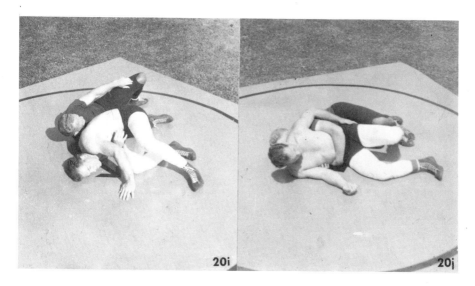

h. RESWITCH.   As B applies the leverage for the switch, A steps up on his left foot, moving his right knee in close to B to catch B's right arm in his crotch.   A is now ready to turn his right toe in and swing his right leg under him to sit through behind B.

i. SIT.   A swings his right leg through, behind B, dragging B's right arm with it and sitting through to his right hip, close behind B, who is pulled down onto his right shoulder by this action.

j. RECOVER.   A reaches his left arm around B's waist and jerks his right arm loose from under B.   As A swings his right leg backward under his left

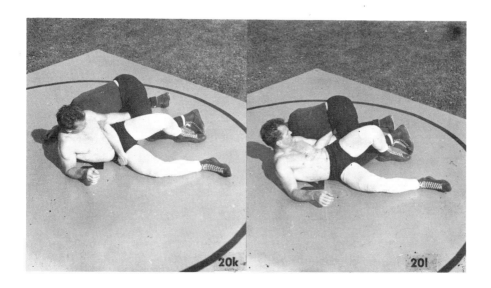

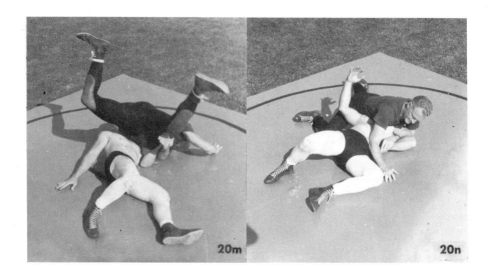

to recover to his knees, B places his left hand on his buttock and prepares to swing his hips away from A for a left-handed switch.

k. LEFT-HANDED SWITCH.   As A recovers to his knees, B extends his left hand into A's crotch by raising up on his right elbow and turning on his buttocks into a sitting position for a left-handed switch.

l. LOCK ARM.   As B applies the leverage against A's right arm, A reaches his left arm backward around B's left arm to lock B's arm into his side and pull B's back toward the mat.

m. SPIN ACROSS.   A swings his left leg across B and follows with his right leg as he pivots on his left shoulder, pushing on mat with right hand. A keeps B's left arm locked under him, pulling B's left shoulder into the mat as he spins across B to the far side.

n. POSITION.   A locks B's left hand under B's back by holding B's left wrist with his left hand as he braces his right hand on the mat to balance his weight across B's chest. A can proceed into a key lock from this position (see maneuver 9, illustrations f, g, h, and i).

21. OVERHOOK AND HIP THROW FROM UNDERNEATH TO REVERSE NELSON

a. START.   A and B are in referee's position. A is underneath and B is on top with his right arm around A's waist.

b. OVERHOOK ARM.   A raises his left arm and rotates it backward over B's right arm near the shoulder, hooking B's arm in the crook of his elbow

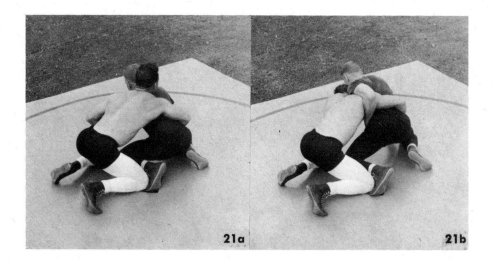

and pulling B's arm up and into him. A keeps his right arm flexed at the elbow and his right hand clenched into his waist.

c. STEP.   A steps his left foot across under B as he pulls B's right arm up and into him.

d. THROW.   A puts his left knee on the mat to rotate his hip in and under B as far as possible, pulling B up and over his left leg and hip. As A drives off his right foot, he continues to pull up and in on B's right arm, starting B off balance by rolling him off the hip toward the mat.

e. RECOVER.   As B falls to the mat, A recovers in a circular motion around B's head and drops his left hand back of B's head for a nelson.

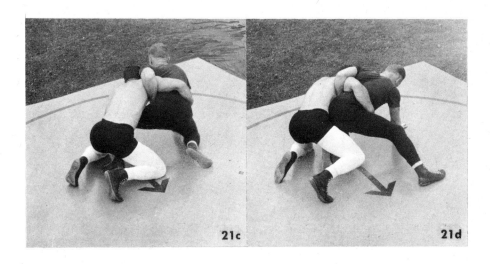

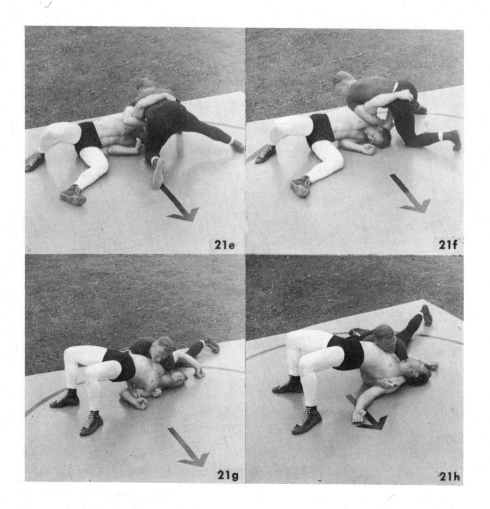

f. SET HEAD.   A sets the nelson by pushing B's head down and in with his right hand as he continues the movement around B's head.

g. DEEP, REVERSE NELSON.   As A moves on behind B, he slides his left arm in for a deep reverse nelson. When B bridges, A reaches under B's back with his right arm so as to hook his hand into his left hand.

h. PIN.   A hooks his hands together and flexes his arms to pull B in snugly. A extends his left leg and bends his right knee, keeping his center of gravity close to the mat as he pulls B in close and under his chest.

22. NEAR LEG PICK-UP AND FORWARD TRIP AGAINST STAND-UP TO ALL FOURS

a. START.   From the referee's position, with B underneath and A on top, B extends his arms and legs to buck into a position on his hands and feet. A steps his right leg in back of B between B's legs, keeping a tight waist hold with his right arm and pressing his right side against B's left hip.

b. HOOK ANKLE.   A removes his left hand from B's left elbow and hooks it inside B's left ankle as he continues to press his right side against B's left hip.

c. PICK UP LEG.   As A pushes B with his right side, he picks up B's left leg, placing it high on his left thigh and close to his waist.

d. LOCK LEG.   A locks his left arm around B's left leg above the knee and steps his right leg in front of B's right leg.

e. TRIP.   A continues to press his right side against B and uses his right leg to trip B's right leg as he follows through to the mat onto his right knee.

f. SPLIT.   A keeps his right knee on the mat and pushed against B's right thigh as he steps toward B's head with his left foot, keeping B's leg high on

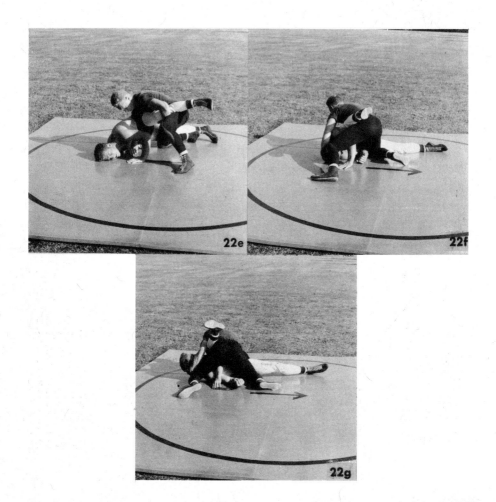

his thigh and locked in the angle between his waist and thigh. A keeps his weight back over his legs and spreads B's legs apart by keeping his right knee set against B's right thigh as he presses B's left leg down against B's left shoulder.

g. PIN. A hooks his left hand under B's head in a reverse nelson position and continues to press down on B's left leg as he twists B's head. A must be careful not to exert too much leverage in twisting B's head or stretching B's legs beyond their normal limits.

23. NEAR-LEG PICK-UP AND BACKWARD DROP

a. START. From the referee's position, with B underneath and A on top, B bucks into a position on his hands and feet as in maneuver 22a. A steps his right leg in back of B between B's legs, keeping his right side against B's left hip and his head down against B's left arm as he removes his left hand from B's left elbow to hook the inside of B's left ankle as in maneuver 22b.

b. DROP.   If B pushes back and raises up to gain a standing position, A pulls down with his right hand on B's right hip and sits through onto his own right hip, under B's left leg, to pivot B to the right and down to the mat.

c. PIVOT.   As A sits through with a pivot motion on his right hip, he lifts up on B's ankle to turn B to the mat on his right side.

d. RECOVER.   A recovers to his knees by stepping forward with his left foot and turning off his right elbow onto his toes to set his knees wide for a good base.

e. STACK-UP RIDE.   A drops into a stack-up ride.   His left arm is between B's legs with the elbow on the mat and his hand hooked under B's right leg. A sits back with his weight over his legs, maintaining good stability by keeping his knees wide, toes turned out, and his right hand braced on the mat in back of B.   A presses the side of his left leg against the lower part of B's left leg to force it against the back of A's left arm, where it is wedged by the downward pressure of A's chest.   A must keep his head in front of B and keep his left elbow bent and on the mat to prevent B from stepping over or switching.

f. LIFT.   A pulls B's legs together with his left arm and lifts them onto his left thigh as he steps up on his left foot, forcing his thigh against the back of

23e   23f

23g

B's legs while using his right hand to grasp B's left arm above the elbow to hold it in place.

g. LEVERAGE.   In order to put B on his back, it may be necessary for A to place his right elbow against the left side of B and lock his right hand into his left hand to provide the leverage against B's side and leg to force B onto his back.

h. REVERSE NELSON.   As B drops to his back, A reaches his right arm under B's neck for a reverse nelson and continues to force B's leg toward his chest.

i. CRADLE.   A locks his hands together for a reverse nelson cradle as he moves around at right angles to B, blocking B's left arm with his right hip.

24. TIGHT WAIST AND HEAD PRY TO HAMMER-LOCK AND HALF-NELSON PIN

a. START.   From the referee's position, with B underneath and A on top, A slides his left hand down B's left arm to hook the front of B's left wrist as he sets the top of his head against the back of B's upper left arm in the arm-pit. A keeps a tight waist hold with his right arm around B and steps his right leg in back of B, with his right thigh pushing up against B's buttocks.

b. LEVERAGE.   With his head wedged against the back of B's upper arm, A pulls back on B's left wrist to remove B's left arm as a support. At the same time A uses his right arm and body weight to pull B to the left and forward onto his left shoulder on the mat.

c. HAMMER LOCK.   A retains a "shake hands" grip with his left hand on B's left wrist and pulls B's left arm behind his back into a hammer-lock posi-

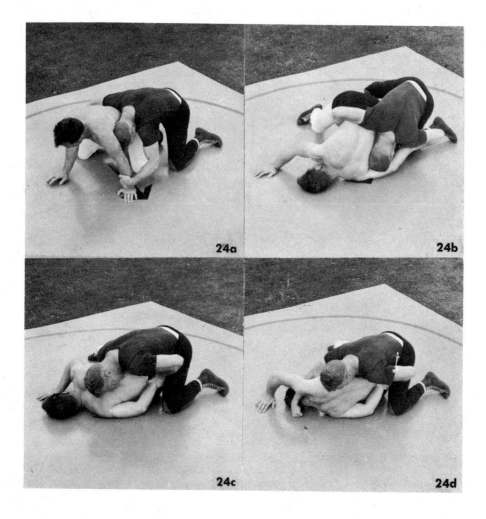

tion. A supports this hammer lock with his left thigh and keeps his right hand locked around B's waist.

d. HALF NELSON. A retains the hammer lock with his left hand and thrusts his right arm under B's right arm, placing his fist against the back of B's head to set B's head in a half nelson.

e. DEEP HALF NELSON. Retaining the hammer lock and keeping the leverage on B's head by leaning his weight against B's right arm, A steps in front of B with his right knee on the mat against B's forehead and his left knee on the mat against B's stomach. A sits back on his legs as he slides his right arm around B's neck for a deep half nelson and pulls B's left wrist against his back into the hammer-lock position. Care must be exercised not to pull B's wrist above a right angle to his body or away from his back into a twisting hammer lock, which is illegal.

f. PIN. A pulls B's left arm tight around his back and turns B onto his back by twisting B's head up into his right side and pressing the right side of his neck down against B's right arm. A moves his right knee under B's head and extends his left leg to roll his weight into the lower part of B's chest as he keeps B's head twisted up off the mat.

25. BLOCK HEAD PRY

a. START. A is underneath and B is on top in the head pry position (maneuver 24a). As B slides his left hand down to hook the front of A's left wrist, A bends his left elbow inward and slides his hand outward to prevent B from hooking his left hand on A's wrist.

b. BLOCK. A continues to slide his hand outward until his elbow touches the mat and B's hand slides up to the crook of A's elbow. A has lowered his center of gravity by dropping his chest toward the mat, and he has increased the area of his base by moving his left hand outward, thereby increasing his stability.

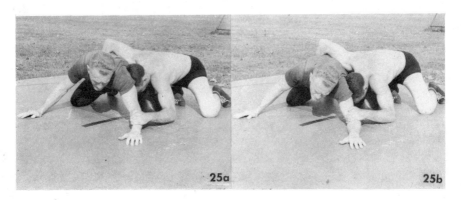

26. BACK HEEL FROM REAR STANDING

a. START: REAR STANDING POSITION.   A is standing behind B. The back of A's right hand is against B's lower abdomen. A hooks his hands together, pulling his right arm around B's abdomen as he presses down on B's hip with his left forearm. A's legs are back, away from B's reach, and are spread in a comfortable position. The right side of A's face is pressed against B's left side just above his hip. B takes hold of A's right hand and pulls up on A's left forearm with his left hand to loosen the pressure of the grip around his waist.

b. JUMP.   A jumps both feet forward, placing his left arch against B's left heel, with his right foot placed inside B's right foot. A has both knees turned out.

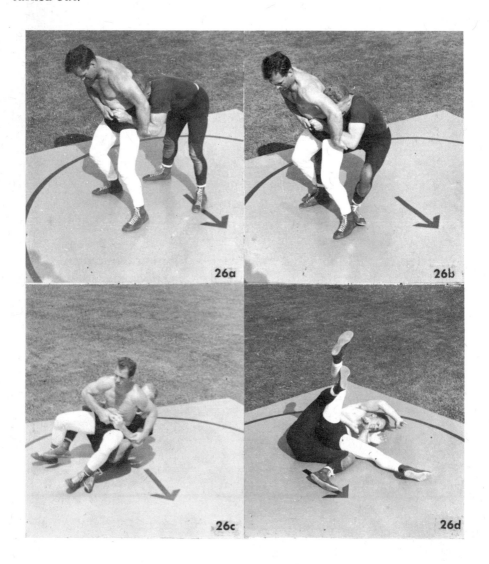

c. SIT.   A sits down as though sitting in a chair and pulls B into his lap. A has both knees outside B's legs as he draws his right instep along under B's right leg, toward the crook of the knee.

d. KICK OVER.   A pulls B to the left and reaches for B's left wrist with both hands as he gives B's right leg a thrust with his right instep to roll B over to the left.

e. RECOVER.   A gets the two-on-one bar on B's left arm as he swings his left leg under his right.   A turns on the balls of his feet, setting his knees out wide as he recovers at right angles to B with the leverage on the two-on-one bar arm (see maneuver 18i and j and maneuver 19a and b, pages 48-49).

f. LEVERAGE.   A straightens his left arm across B's back, pressing his left shoulder into B's right shoulder blade as he pries up with his left hand hooked under the crook of B's left elbow.   A keeps hold of B's right wrist with his right hand and swings his body above a right angle, keeping his knees and toes turned outward as he applies the leverage across B's upper back.

27. SWITCH TO COUNTER BACK HEEL

a. START.   B is behind A in a rear standing position (maneuver 26a). The back of B's right hand is against A's waist, and B's hands are locked in a wrestler's grip with his left arm pressed against A's left hip.   A leans forward with his hands on his knees and most of his weight on his right foot.

b. REACH FOR SWITCH.   As B takes A down with a back heel (maneuvers 26b, c, and d), A reaches his right hand inside B's right leg and swings his buttocks away from B, trying to land in a sitting position on the mat.

c. SIT FOR SWITCH.   As B recovers to his knees, A places the palm of his

right hand against the inside of B's right thigh and continues to swing his buttocks away from B, moving into a sitting position for the switch. By extending his upper body and right arm, A applies pressure to B's right arm near the armpit (maneuvers 18d and e).

d. BREAKDOWN.   A maintains the pressure on B's right arm and swings his buttocks toward his left heel, away from B, to force B to the mat (maneuvers 18e and f).

e. RECOVER.   A steps his left leg over his right leg, turning on his right toe and elbow to a position on top of B with his weight pressed into B (maneuvers 18g and h).

f. TWO-ON-ONE BAR ARM.   As B attempts to recover to his knees, A contacts B's left wrist with both hands and moves across B to apply leverage with the two-on-one bar arm (maneuver 18i).

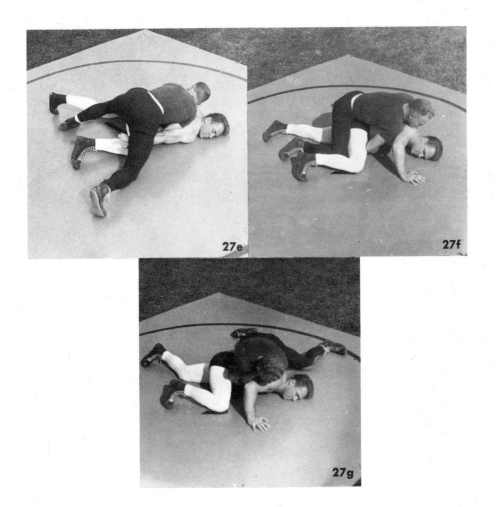

g. LEVERAGE AND POSITION. A's right hand holds B's left wrist, and his left hand is hooked under B's forearm as A leans his left shoulder into B's right shoulder blade to provide leverage that forces up and out on B's left forearm. A's left arm is straight as he pivots on his left shoulder to a position on the left side of B, at right angles to B's back (maneuver 18j).

28. STAND-UP ESCAPE

a. START. A and B are in the referee's position. A is underneath and B is on top with his right arm around A's waist. A pushes on the mat with both hands, forcing his weight back over his legs and pushing the left side of his back into B's chest.

b. TRIPOD POSITION. As B steps his right foot behind A, A continues to force backward into B. A steps up on his right foot to brace against B's force

as he takes hold of B's four fingers in his right hand. He slides his left hand back, alongside his left leg for support, as he raises his left knee off the mat. A also keeps his left arm close to his side to prevent B from locking his left arm around A's waist. A tries to get his center of gravity over the center of his base by turning his hips away from B and raising his left knee up and into B. This action also swings B behind A and relieves the sideward force B has been exerting.

c. **STAND.**   As A rotates his hips away from B, he moves up into a standing position, bracing his left forearm against his left thigh for additional support against B's force. A continues to control B's right hand by holding B's fingers and locking B's arm against his side with his right arm. **B stands** to both feet and moves in close to A, keeping his left hand hooked on A's left arm to keep control of A.

d. WALK-STRIDE POSITION.   As B moves in behind and pulls A in close to his chest, A steps his right foot forward into a walk-stride standing position, keeping control of B's right hand with the grip on B's fingers and the lock on B's arm.   A keeps his left arm bent, with his elbow close to his side, and prevents B from reaching inside or over his arm to lock his hands around A's waist.

e. SWING HIPS FORWARD.   A swings his hips forward away from B as he slips B's right hand up to his armpit and drops his left shoulder under B's chest.

28e   28f

28g

f. TURN.   A lets go of B's hand and reaches for the mat with his right hand as he swings his left arm backward and upward to block B if he tries to move behind.

g. PIVOT AWAY.   A pivots on his right hand and moves his legs away from B as he throws his left arm around B's back to start a crawfish in case B tries to spin behind.   A sets his right knee out and down on the mat to maintain a tripod position with his right hand and left foot.

h. PUSH.   If B makes no move to spin behind, A moves his left hand to B's right thigh and pushes B away to a neutral position.

i. NEUTRAL.   B keeps his distance by pushing on A's shoulders with both hands.   A maintains a good base and keeps his eyes on B's hips.   A is ready to catch B in a crawfish with either arm if B attempts to spin behind.

29. CRAWFISH REVERSAL

a. START.   A is under and B is on top in the referee's position.   A pushes on the mat with both hands, forcing into B to start the stand-up escape (maneuver 28a).   B remains on his knees at the side of A and tries to break A down with a tight waist and arm pull.

b. TRIPOD POSITION (B stays on his knees to left of A).   A braces his right foot on the mat and uses his right hand to grasp the fingers of B's right hand as he continues to push into B with his left side (maneuver 28b).   A uses his left hand on the mat to brace himself against B's force as B continues to try to break A down to his left side.

c. SLIP THE HAND.   As B continues his force to break A down, A lifts outward on B's right hand to loosen it, and slips it upward under his right armpit as he drops his left elbow to the mat, turning his left shoulder in under B's chest.

d. CRAWFISH.   A places his right knee and right hand on the mat, turning in deeper under B's chest as he raises his left knee off the mat to bring his left arm backward from under B, placing it around B's back.

e. BUCK.   A backs out into a buck position and raises his left leg to step across B as he uses his left arm around B to pull B under him.   A keeps his head down and makes a steep slide out of his back so that B's arm will slide down over A's head as A steps across and pulls B under him, as in maneuver 4h, page 21.

f. BREAKDOWN.   A moves into a crotch pry and arm pull to force B down to his right side on the mat (maneuvers 14c and d).

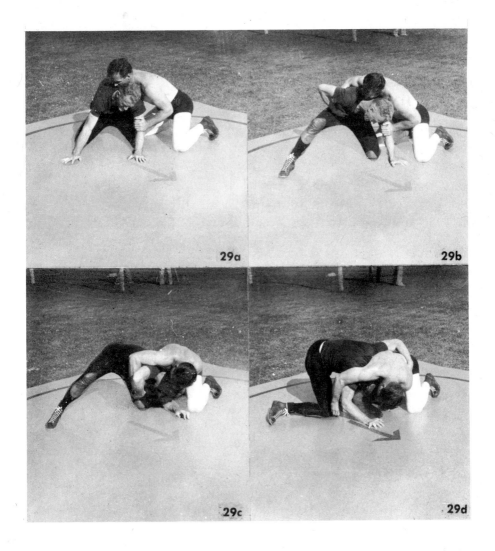

30A. CROSS FACE AGAINST A SINGLE LEG HOLD

a. START.   A is standing and B is on his knees facing A.   B locks his arms around A's right leg with his head to the outside of the leg.

b. BLOCK.   A drops to the mat on his hands and knees at the right side of B.   A's right hand is on the mat under B's face, and his left hand is hooked over B's right ankle, with his arm alongside B's hip.   A sits back on his legs to get his chest under B's side as low as possible.

c. LEVERAGE.   A extends his legs backward, dropping his stomach toward the mat, working his right arm across under B's face, and keeping his left

hand hooked on B's right ankle. B lets go of A's leg with his left hand and puts it on the mat to maintain his balance.

d. STEP OVER LEG. Keeping the leverage across B's face, A continues to move his right leg away from B. As B's right hand starts to slide off A's right leg, A steps his left heel over B's right ankle and draws the ankle to him. This swings B's upper body away from A, causing B's right hand to slip off A's leg as A moves around behind B.

e. LOCK LEG. A locks his left ankle under B's right ankle by sitting back on it. A slides his left arm around B's upper right leg, placing his left hand just above B's right knee as he places his left shoulder under B's right buttock.

30c   30d

30e   30f

f. DRIVE FORWARD.   A pushes with his left shoulder as he pulls B's leg into him with his left hand and raises up on B's right ankle with his left heel. This leverage on B's right leg forces B forward and down to his stomach on the mat.

30B. CROSS FACE INTO BODY-LOCK PIN

g. FAR ARM.   In the block position (maneuver 30b), if B keeps his hands locked around A's right leg when A tries to extend his legs backward (maneuver 30c), A hooks his right hand on B's left triceps and keeps his left hand hooked on B's right ankle.

h. ROLL OVER.   As A tries to extend his legs backward, he pulls on B's left arm and picks up B's right ankle, turning B onto his left shoulder.

i. LOCK WAIST.   A pulls B's left arm up under his right arm, and as B rolls to his left side, A locks his left arm around B's back. A sits on his left buttock, moving his legs into a running-stride position, with the left leg forward.

j. LOCK ARMS.   A continues to pull up on B's left arm and locks both of B's arms under his right arm as he moves his left arm deep around B's back. As B bridges to the left, A pulls up on B's left arm and pushes his left side into B's chest.

k. TIGHTEN BODY LOCK.   As B bridges to the right, A tightens his left arm around B's back, dropping his weight back to his left hip on the mat. A locks B's arms tight to his side under his right arm. Should A lose his balance across B, he lets go of B's arms and turns onto his stomach, getting

a reverse nelson with his right arm as he maintains the waist lock with his left arm.

31. STAND-UP COUNTER AGAINST CROSS-FACE

a. START. A is on his hands and knees and B is on top in a cross-face position. B's right hand is hooked on A's left triceps, and B's left hand is hooked over A's right ankle. B's left knee is on the mat and his right foot is braced on the mat to his right side.

b. CONTROL ARM AND STEP UP. A uses his left hand to grasp B's right triceps and steps up toward B on his left foot to raise B upward as he pulls

in on B's arm to control it. A drops his right shoulder under B's chest as he centers his weight over his right knee and turns his chest toward B's chest.

c. RIGHT ARM AROUND. As A gets his chest under B's chest, he reaches his right arm around B's back, hooking his fingers into the middle of B's back as he steps closer to B with his left foot. B keeps his left hand hooked on A's right ankle.

d. BEAR HUG. A releases B's right arm and reaches his left arm around B's back, hooking the fingers of his left hand into the middle of B's back. By pulling in on B's back with both hands and pushing with his chest under B's chest, A straightens B up, causing B's left hand to slip up A's right leg as

A starts to raise his right knee off the mat and turn it outward to step up on his right foot.

e. WALK OVER HIM. A steps up on his right foot toward B, pulling B into him with the bear hug leverage described in (d). A walks into B and attempts to bend B over backward.

f. BEND HIM BACKWARD. If B stands up, A continues to pull in on B's back with both hands and to push his chest up against B's chest, pulling B into his stomach as he walks into B and bends B backward to the mat.

NOTE: The stand-up counter against the cross-face can be added to the spinning drill. On the command "cross face," given during the spinning exercise, the top man moves into the cross-face position as described in 31a. The bottom man immediately reacts against the cross-face with the stand-up counter, 31b to 31f inclusive. On the command "spin," the two men resume the spinning exercise.

32. RELEASE FAR ANKLE AND SIT OUT

a. START. A is underneath and B is on top with his right hand hooked on A's right ankle and his left hooked in the crook of A's left elbow (maneuver 11b). A pushes on the mat with both hands to force his back under B's right arm as far as possible.

b. STRAIGHT ARM AND EXTEND THE LEG. A uses his right hand to take hold of B's right wrist, pushing B's wrist outward with a straight right arm as he extends his right leg to the side and moves his ankle beyond B's grasp by keeping his body between B and the ankle. A is sitting on his left leg with his left toe turned in, ready for a sit out. It may be necessary for A to move into a position on his left hip in order to extend the leg sufficiently to release B's grasp.

c. SIT.   A swings his left leg under his right leg and drives off from his left hand, pushing B's right arm backward as he slides into an extended position on his left side.

d. ROLL OVER.   A rolls to the left, bringing his right knee up on the mat to recover to a position on both knees.

e. RECOVER.   A pulls his left knee up and under him, setting it wide as he pushes on the mat with his hands to a position on his hands and knees.

f. ARM JERK.   A hooks his left hand on B's left arm just under the arm-

pit and jerks B forward as he steps up on his right foot alongside of B to go behind him.

g. SPIN. A spins behind B into a floating position on top as B pushes back to recover from the arm jerk.

33. DOUBLE LEG TACKLE TO HALF NELSON CRADLE

a. START. Both wrestlers are standing face to face. B hooks his right hand on A's neck. A takes hold of B's right triceps with his left hand, pulling B's arm into a flexed position against A's left shoulder. A places his forehead against B's right collarbone and reaches his right arm under B's left arm, hooking his hand on B's left shoulder blade. A pushes against B to get B forcing into him.

b. STEP IN AND DROP TO KNEE.   As B forces into A, A takes a short step forward with his right foot, drops to his right knee, and pulls B down onto A's right shoulder and across his neck.   A must keep his right toe turned out to maintain a good base for balance.

c. TACKLE POSITION ON RIGHT KNEE.   A remains on his right knee and steps forward on his left foot, reaching as far as he can reach around B's legs with both arms to pull B's legs in tight against A's chest and abdomen.

d. LIFT.   A straightens up to lift B off the mat, holding him draped over the shoulder like a sack of wheat.   A pulls B's legs together by reaching as far as he can reach around B's legs.   A keeps his right toe turned out to maintain his balance as he holds B on his shoulder.

e. TAKEDOWN.   A swings B's legs over his left leg and sets B down on the mat to the right, keeping his right toe turned out and his knee on the mat

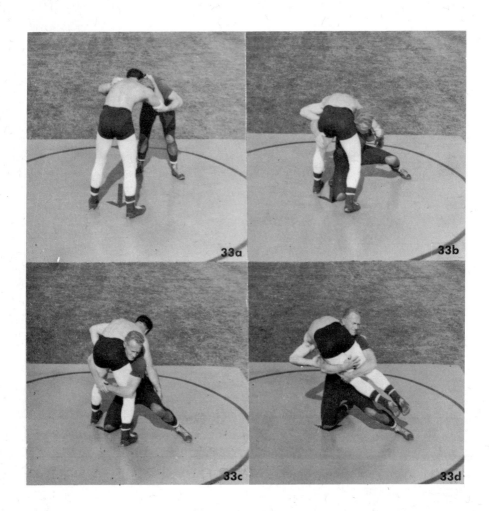

for balance. A keeps B's legs pulled in close to his side and supports them on his left thigh.

f. HALF NELSON. A overhooks his right arm around B's neck for a deep half nelson as he pulls B's legs up toward B's chest.

g. CRADLE. A lets go of B's left leg and pulls B's right leg into B's chest. A hooks the fingers of his right hand into the fingers of his left hand for a cradle hold. A is on both knees and lifts B's head into his side.

h. PIN. A extends his right leg and presses his right side down on B's head. A flexes both arms, pulling his elbows into his sides, and leans all his weight onto B's head. This pulls B's right leg down to B's chest and exerts a great deal of pressure on B's head to hold him on his back in a very tight pinning position.

34. COUNTER SIDE-HEAD LOCK WITH BACKWARD DROP

a. START: COLLAR-ELBOW POSITION. Each wrestler has his forehead against the collarbone of his adversary, with his right hand hooked on the neck and his left holding the triceps.

b. HEAD LOCK. B steps forward with his right foot, reaching around A's neck with his right arm and turning his hips under A. A hooks B's left arm with both hands pulling B in close to him as A moves his left leg under B and brings his right foot along the outside of B's right foot. A bends his knees into a partial squat position as he raises his head up and bulls his neck against the force of the head lock.

c. LIFT. A lifts B off the mat by holding B tight against his abdomen as he straightens his legs, raises his head up, and leans back to support B against his abdomen.

d. SIT. A sits down as though sitting in a chair. A's knees are bent and outside B's legs. A keeps B pulled into his lap until he hits the mat.

e. **RECOVER.** As A sits on the mat, he rolls B to the left, recovering at right angles to B with his legs extended and his hands braced on the mat to counteract the force of B's head lock, which he maintains. A rests his chin against the right side of B's chest.

f. **HEAD UP.** When B eases up on the head lock, A extends his head upward under B's right arm and steps over B's legs as he starts the pivot to move in front of B.

g. **MOVE ACROSS.** A continues to pivot across B until his chest is pressing against B's chest. A's head remains extended upward and his hands and feet are braced on the mat for balance.

h. **HALF NELSON.** A overhooks his right arm around B's neck for a half nelson as he gets an inside crotch hold with his left hand and balances on top of B in the toe-chest position.

35. ARM-DRAG COUNTER AGAINST SINGLE LEG PICK-UP

a. START.   A is standing and B is on his knees facing A. B anchors both arms around A's right leg, with his head outside A's leg. B pulls A's leg in close to his chest.

b. BLOCK.   A drops to his hands and knees at the side of B to block the leg tackle with a cross-face (see maneuver 30, Cross-Face Against Single Leg Hold). B keeps A's leg locked tight with his arms and moves in close to A's right leg to pick it up.

c. HOOK ARM AND LEG.   B steps up on his left foot and pulls A's right leg in close to his chest as he moves in to pick up A's right leg. A hooks his right hand on B's right arm just under the armpit and hooks his left hand on B's right leg just under B's right buttock. A pulls B's right shoulder in close to the right side of his abdomen as he leans his weight onto his right foot and

onto B's right shoulder, keeping B's arms pulled up above A's right knee, which is bent into B.

d. HOOK INSTEP. As B stands up with A's right leg, A extends his leg through B's arms and hooks his right instep in the crook of B's left knee. A keeps his right hand hooked on B's triceps and presses his own right forearm and elbow into his side to keep B's right arm pulled in close to the right side of A's abdomen. A lifts on B's left leg with his left hand, which is hooked just below B's left buttock. A presses the right side of his face against B's right shoulder blade and keeps B pulled in close to him.

e. PRESS DOWN. A pivots on his left foot as he extends his right leg downward, sliding his right instep down B's left leg and keeping B pulled in close. A presses down on B's right shoulder and shoulder blade with his chest

and head, respectively.   It is very important that A keep B's arms locked into his side and that A fall on his right side as he presses B down with him.

f. HOLD.   As A falls on his right side, he keeps his right leg extended through the crook of B's left knee.   A continues to keep B's right arm locked tight under his side as he presses his head and chest down on B's right scapula and shoulder, respectively.   A also continues to pull B's right leg in close to him with the outside crotch hold he has with his left hand.   A's left foot remains on the mat as a pivot to swing his hips out from under B.

g. RECOVER.   A places his right hand on the mat near B's head and pivots on his right hand and left foot as he lifts up on B's right leg to swing his own right leg back under his left, extending it away from B as in the cross-face, maneuver 30b.

h. LEVERAGE.   A extends his legs backward, dropping his stomach toward the mat, working his right arm under B's face, and keeping his left hand hooked on B's right leg.

i. STEP OVER LEG.   A moves his right leg away from B and steps his left heel over B's right ankle, drawing the ankle to him with his heel as he moves behind B.

j. CONTROL.   A steps into a floating position on top of B, forcing B forward.

36. UNDERARM SNEAK

a. START.   Both wrestlers are standing face to face.   A takes hold of B's arms just below the shoulder, keeping his arms straight as he pushes against B.   B takes hold of A's triceps, pulling up and in on A's arms and trying to bend them.

b. STEP IN AND DROP KNEE TOWARD MAT. A overhooks B's left arm with his right hand as he takes a short step forward with his right foot and drops his right knee toward the mat, stepping to the left with his left foot as he raises B's right arm outward to duck under it.

c. PULL DOWN AND OVER. A keeps hold of B's right arm, pulling it out and down until B is pulled over A's right shoulder and against the right side of A's neck. A keeps his right hand overhooked on B's left arm, pulling down and in on the arm as he reaches around B's hips with his left arm. A's right knee is close to the mat and may touch it lightly in this position. The right side of A's head and neck is pressed tightly against B's side.

d. UP. A continues pulling down and in on B's left arm and steps up to a standing position close to the right side of B as he reaches his left arm around B's back, hooking his left hand on his right wrist. As A pulls B

36a   36b

36c   36d

tightly into him, he moves in close as though about to pick up B against his abdomen.

e. SHUFFLE BEHIND.   A eases up just enough on the body hold to shuffle behind B, where he again tightens up on the lock around B's body.   Note that A's right hand remains hooked on B's left arm, and A's left hand is hooked on the top of his own right wrist.   A pulls down and in on B's left arm to keep B's left arm locked against his side.   A moves in close against B, keeping his knees bent and getting his abdomen under B's buttocks for the lift.

f. LIFT.   A leans back as he straightens his legs and supports B against his abdomen to lift him off the mat.

g. SIT.   A starts to sit down as though sitting in a chair, bending his knees wide to pull B into his lap.

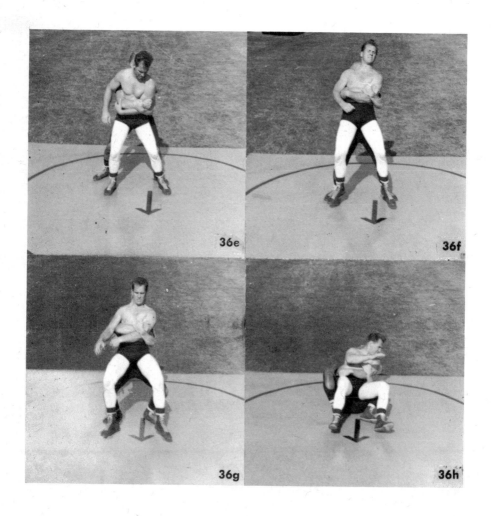

h. PULL INTO LAP. A pulls B into his lap as he sits on the mat, and hooks his right instep under the crook of B's right knee as he gets ready to roll B to the left.

i. ROLL. A pulls B to the left and gives B's right leg a thrust with his right instep as he unhooks his hands from B's arm to hook both hands on B's left wrist, for a two-on-one bar arm.

j. RECOVER TO TWO-ON-ONE BAR ARM. A swings his left leg under his right leg and recovers at right angles to B, with the two-on-one leverage on B's left arm and across B's upper back. See maneuver 26f.

37. STRETCHER TO FRONT-BODY SCISSORS, OR LEG GRAPEVINE

a. START. From the referee's position on the mat (B down, A on top), A moves into a floating position and uses his right forearm to block against the back of B's right arm, keeping a space between B's right arm and right leg.

b. BLOCK AND STEP RIGHT FOOT IN. A steps his right foot in between B's knees as A blocks B's right arm.

c. BLOCK AND STEP LEFT FOOT IN. A blocks B's left arm with his left arm as he steps his left foot in between B's knees. A's knees are turned out, and his abdomen and chest are pressed down on B's back.

d. TAKE HOLD OF WRISTS. A removes his arms from behind B's arms and takes hold of the front of B's wrists as he drops more of his chest on to B's back and moves his feet in deeper between B's legs.

e. BREAKDOWN.   A picks up on B's wrists as he raises his heels up between B's legs and increases the leverage on B's back by raising his chest and dropping his abdomen into the middle of B's back.   A hooks an instep of one foot over the heel of his other foot and keeps his heels raised in the air. This action raises B's legs off the mat, forcing B's chest into the mat.

f. LEVERAGE.   A sets his knees wide on the mat as he pushes back, raising his chest up and dropping his lower abdomen into the small of B's back.   A keeps his instep hooked over his heel and his heels raised in the air.   This keeps B's legs in the air and his chest forced into the mat.

g. HALF NELSON. A pulls B's right arm up alongside of B's head and pushes on B's head with his left hand as he gets a half nelson with his right. A unhooks his instep from B's heel and starts to turn B over with the leverage from the half nelson. A keeps his knees wide and his heels on the mat, digging his heels into and under B's legs as he turns B over.

h. DEEP HALF NELSON. As B is turned to his back, A slips his right arm deep around B's neck for a deep half nelson. A keeps his knees wide on the mat and digs his heels under B's legs as he picks up B's head. A presses his abdomen into the lower part of B's chest and uses his left hand on the mat for balance, to help raise his chest up as he twists B's head into his side.

i. HOOK INSTEP OVER HEEL. A hooks his right instep over his own left heel and raises his heels as high as possible to force B's back into the mat as he continues the leverage on B's chest and neck.

j. HOOK INSTEPS ON ANKLES. When B tries to bridge, A extends his legs between B's legs, hooking his insteps on B's ankles. As A extends his legs in this position, he exerts a great deal of leverage on B's legs. At the same time A maintains the deep half nelson and pressure on B's chest.

k. REHOOK INSTEP OVER HEEL. If B can extend his legs and force A to unhook his insteps, A will rehook his instep over his heel as he returns to position (i). If B gets his legs in bridging position again, A should again hook his insteps on B's ankles for the double-leg grapevine, as in position (j).

38. CROSS-BODY RIDE TO GUILLOTINE

a. START. From the referee's position on the mat (B down, A on top), A moves into a floating position and uses his right forearm against the back of

B's right arm to block B's arm and keep a space between B's right arm and leg for A to put his leg through.

b. CROSS-BODY RIDE POSITION.   A steps his right foot in between B's knees and swings his body across B's back, hooking his right elbow into B's left armpit and hooking B's left ankle with his left hand.   A moves his right leg between B's legs, hooking his right instep over B's right ankle.   A leans across the lower part of B's back, forcing his right hip into the small of B's back and keeping his left foot on the mat in back of B for balance.

c. UNDERHOOK.   A reaches his right arm under B's left arm, to quickly hook B's left arm and jerk it back into B's side.

d. ELBOW IN BACK.   A continues the pull on B's left arm, using his left hand to help bring B's left arm up so A can get his right elbow in the middle of B's back.

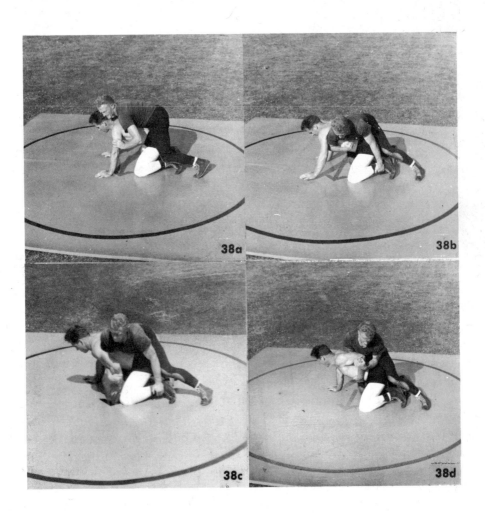

e. **LEVERAGE.**   A pushes his right elbow into B's back as he continues to pull on B's left elbow, with both hands forcing B to roll over onto his right side.

f. **HOOK LEGS.**   As B falls to his right side, A hooks his right instep in the crook of his left knee and hooks his left instep under B's right ankle, keeping control of B's left arm with both hands.

g. **ARM UNDER BACK.**   A raises B's left arm over his head and under his back as he cuts down on B's right leg by extending both of his legs and forcing his abdomen against B's buttocks.

h. **LOCK.**   A locks both hands on B's head and pulls the head into him as he continues to apply the leverage on B's right leg with just enough force to keep B from moving.   A must be careful not to pull on the head and squeeze the leg too hard, as it becomes a punishing hold and can be illegal. *Note:* Under interscholastic rules it is illegal to lock or overlap the hands or arms around an opponent's head or neck in securing this hold.

4

Summary of Holds
and Maneuvers

This summary classifies holds and maneuvers according to their functions. The number listed with each refers to the maneuver where the action is described and illustrated.

ESCAPES AND REVERSALS

Escapes to neutral
  Sit-out and turn-in, 4
  Sit-out and turn-out, 17
  Stand-up, 28
  Release for ankle and sit-out, 32

Reversals
  Crawfish, 4, 5, 28, 29
  Far-side roll, 13, 20c
  Switch, 18, 20a, 20c, 20g, 27
  Overhook and hip throw, 21

Counters for common methods of escapes and reversals
  Overdrag against sit-out and turn-in, 15
  Breakdowns, 11
  Roll-through, 20d
  Reswitch, 20f
  Lock arm and spin across switch, 20h

RIDES

Breakdowns and control positions
  Tight waist, 7, 11a, 24, 20b
  Bar arm and outside crotch, 8, 14
  Far ankle and near-arm pull, 11b
  Inside crotch pry and near-arm pull, 11c, 14

Rear standing
   Near-leg pick-up and forward trip, 22
   Near-leg pick-up and backward drop, 23
   Back heel, 26
   Backward drop against side head lock, 34
   Arm lock and body lift to backward drop, 36

Front standing
   Bear hug, 31
   Double leg tackle, 33
   Single leg pick-up, 35
   Arm drag, 35
   Underarm sneak, 36

Takedown counters and blocks
   Crawfish against spins from neutral, 4, 5, 28
   Double underhooks, 12
   Switch to counter back heel, 27
   Cross-face, 30
   Stand-up against cross-face, 31
   Counter side head with backward drop, 34
   Arm drag counter against single leg pick-up, 35

5

Wrestling Analyzed

Proficiency in sports is essentially and directly related to mechanical competence in the execution of motor skills and techniques. The laws of physics provide the basic principles to interpret the correct procedure for executing these skills and techniques. The following list of essential rules of action * for wrestling indicates the relationship of these mechanical principles to efficient movement and control in this sport. This information, with the scientific assurance that the correct fundamentals are provided, will have an extremely favorable effect on the confidence and interest of the coaches and participants as well as on their proficiency.

ESSENTIAL RULES OF ACTION

Timing. The most effective time to make a throw or move is when your opponent is exerting force or moving in the desired direction.

Feinting. A deceptive movement is the essence of strategy in getting your opponent to exert force or to move in a desired direction. Whether it be a direct attack or a counter movement, the action is best made under the guise of a feint. The feint is a short movement under control that induces a long movement by the adversary which jeopardizes his equilibrium.

Continuity of Maneuvers. A direct attack rarely succeeds. The aggressor whose initial maneuver fails should follow with a second maneuver immediately, and if this fails, still another maneuver may be tried and so on. The anticipation and preparation of the opponent to stop the attack will be found to decrease with each trial, and the possibility of success by the aggressor will increase accordingly.

Combination Holds. In order to control an opponent in any position, it is usually necessary to apply a hold with each hand. The ability to control an opponent can be further enhanced by applying holds with the legs along with the holds applied by the hands.

* Hugh F. Leonard, *A Handbook of Wrestling* (New York: E. R. Pelton, Publisher, 1897), Chapter 2.

Centering the Weight.   When down on the mat, each wrestler should use his body weight to its greatest advantage, to prevent the action of his opponent.   The top man centers his weight on the bottom man to keep him forced down on the mat and to change holds when it is necessary.   When the top man seeks to lift the bottom man or to pull him into a greater position of jeopardy, the bottom man centers his weight as far as possible from the spot at which the top man is lifting or pulling.

Leverage and Direction of Force.   To turn an opponent onto his back with a hold on the arm, it is desirable to push his arm above his head, with the force applied toward the outer end of the arm away from the armpit in order to secure the advantage of a long lever arm.   As in the case of a half nelson, the force is applied diagonally forward against the arm near the elbow and *not* perpendicularly to the long axis of the body of the opponent.   The object is not to roll him upon his back but to turn him squarely upon both shoulder blades.   The force is also being applied upon the head instead of the neck, where the effect is needed.

Blocking the Leverage.   The shorter the neck, the less is the leverage to be obtained on it.   Drawing the neck in between the shoulders shortens it as much as possible.   Locking the opponent's arm above his elbow, and pulling it down and into the the side, reduces the leverage of the nelson, controls the arm, and pulls the hand off the head to the side of the neck, thereby minimizing the leverage in the nelson.

The Neck.   When the neck becomes flexed and twisted, its resistant power is lost.   An effective pinning combination wedges the head in a flexed and twisted position.   To resist any position where the force comes upon the neck, as in bridging and in the application of nelsons, the neck should be drawn in between the shoulders to make the neck and body as one unit.

The Thumb (Gripping).   In securing holds with the hand, the thumb should be used as a fifth finger alongside the other fingers when they are hooked onto a part.   This greatly increases the holding power of the hand.

The Back (Lifting).   In order to execute an effective lift on an opponent, the back should be as stiff as possible, and the force should be applied through the use of the legs.

The Arms.   Allowing the arms to hang loosely over an opponent provides an opportunity for them to be seized and pulled in under him as he rolls to his side, resulting in getting pulled under into a near-fall position.   The elbows should always be kept in close to the sides to prevent effectively the holds that result in pinning situations.

The Eyes and Sense of Touch.   Each wrestler should keep his eyes constantly fastened on the actions of his adversary.   When the adversary is out of view, the sense of touch must be used to determine what the opponent is trying to do.

Explosiveness.   All action should be executed with vim and snap, whether it be an attack or defensive movement. Slowness usually results in failure.

Relaxation.   Rigidity of pose and constant use of strength induce fatigue and inhibit reactions. Quickness and endurance are enhanced when the antagonistic muscles in the arms and legs are slightly stretched without rigidity and are ready to provide movement in any direction.

Movement Underneath.   The wrestler underneath on the mat should maneuver constantly to prevent his adversary from securing a hold with deliberation, and he should also afford himself an opportunity to attain a maneuver that may lead to his escape. When in doubt as to how to escape, always try to stand up, controlling opponent's hands and keeping them apart. Never lie on your stomach when you can get to your knees, and never stay on your knees when you can get to your feet.

Bump when in Doubt.   When an adversary is gaining an advantage in a maneuver and there is some doubt as to a counterattack, drive against him with a sudden thrust. The bump will usually throw him off balance enough to loosen the hold and permit a recovery for the counterattack.

6

Outline for Thirty Lessons

LESSON I

CHECKING IN. *Weigh in* all men in uniform (sweat clothes, shoes, overtrunks). Class forms line in alphabetical order. The weights are recorded in roll book.

INTRODUCTORY REMARKS

Briefly discuss wrestling and demonstrate the essential items in a match.

Emphasize contribution to growth and development including carryover and continuing values.

Clarify various styles of wrestling:

Professional, school and college, Olympic, AAU, and Greco Roman.

Essential items: Takedown, Reversal, Escape, Near Fall, Fall, Time Advantage (NCAA Guide, Rules 8 and 9).

CLASS REGULATIONS

Uniform is mandatory; consists of sweat suit, overtrunks, supporter, socks, and shoes.

Attendance and excuses. Outline departmental policies.

Class marks:

Checkouts 50 per cent, includes attitudes, interest, skill, rules, and leadership.

Competition 50 per cent, includes skill, vigor, and strategy.

Safety precautions:

No jewelry, finger nails trimmed, care of abrasions.

Report chronic injuries and colds.

CLASS FORMATION

Size off by weights along edge of mat, space equidistant apart, and count off by fours.

Open ranks (each takes twice the number of steps as their number).

Even numbers about face and move to left in front of odd numbers to form partners.

All face instructor for individual mass drill.

101

WARM-UP ACTIVITIES.   Class is in open formation.

I. *Mat Drill*

On guard position,* I(a) and (b)

Spot running, I(c)

Block, I(d); position, I(e); up, I(f) and g); spot run, I(g).

Buck, I(h); down, I(i).

Backs, I(o); bridging, II(1a) and (b); back push-ups, II(1c)

Bridging right and left, I(o) to (r); with spot running, I(c).

Front, I(i); cuddle right and left, I(j); recover, I(k) to (n).

Push-ups from "Front" position.

Knees bending and stretching exercise

    Start: standing, feet sideways, hands on hips.

    Action: Bend knees to kneeling position on mat and return to
       standing.

       Defensive referee's position on mat I(e):

       From the kneeling position in this exercise place the hands
       on the mat 1 foot in front of the knees.

Sit-out and turn-in (see maneuver 4):

    Start in defensive referee's position I(e).

    Action is same as for (a) in maneuver 4.

LESSON II

Weigh delinquents who were absent first day. Review warm-up drill
from Lesson I. Spinning II 2(a) and (b).

  *1. Block quarter nelson, both sides. (Drill on neck flexion and extension
    against passive resistance.)

  2. Block three-quarter nelson, both sides.

  3. Knee recovery from prone position.

Scrimmage from clam-up position 3(a). Bottom man recovers against resistance 3(b) to (d). Top man exerts full force from balanced floating position 3(b) to d).

LESSON III

Review warm-up drill.

Review spinning.

Review quarter nelson and three-quarter nelson blocking drills.

Review knee recovery from prone position.

Sit-out and turn-in, with top man following in floating position. II(3).

Scrimmage sit-out and turn-in, with top man in floating position.

Bridge over drill with partner. (Reversals from arm lock and body lock
    pin.) II(4).

---

* Roman numerals refer to maneuvers described and illustrated in Chapter 2; Arabic numerals
to those in Chapter 3.

LESSON IV

Warm-up: mat drill, spinning, and bridge over reversals.

4. Sit-out and turn-in to crawfish.

5. Escape to neutral from half nelson and crotch pin.

Scrimmage from half nelson and crotch pin (four 20-sec. periods).

Scoring: One point for maintaining pinning position or one point for getting off back. Stop match if bottom man gets out of pinning situation.

LESSON V

Warm-up: mat drill, spinning.

Review sit-out and turn-in to crawfish.

Review escape to neutral from half nelson and crotch pin. Add crawfish against spin around.

6. Escape (recover) from reverse nelson and crotch pin.

Scrimmage from reverse nelson and crotch pin (four 20-sec. periods).

Scoring: One point for maintaining pinning position or one point for getting off back. Stop match if bottom man gets out of pinning situation.

LESSON VI

Warm-up: spinning, sit-out and turn-in top man follow.

Review escape from half nelson pin with crawfish to top position.

Review escape from reverse nelson and crotch pin.

Review knee recovery from prone position. Add top man trying for a bar arm.

Block half nelson with an elbow-lock roll (see start of No. 9), with top man blocking the roll by stepping across to far side and bracing against arm lock.

7. Release for tight waist ride.

Scrimmage from tight waist-ride position (four 20-sec. periods).

Scoring: One point for maintaining the ride or one point for recovering to knees. If bottom man gets to knees, top man keeps trying to break him down again until end of period.

LESSON VII

Warm-up: sit-out and turn-in, recovery from prone position. Escape half nelson and reverse nelson pins.

Review release for tight waist ride.

8. Release for bar arm and outside crotch.

9. Block near-side half nelson with elbow-lock roll to key lock.

Explain all nelsons 2, 3, and 9 including illegal full nelson (NCAA Guide, Rule 10).

Scrimmage from bar arm and outside crotch position (six 15-sec. periods).

Scoring: One point for maintaining position on top or one point for releasing wrist and recovering to knees.

LESSON VIII

Warm-up: spinning, recovery from prone position, release tight waist ride, release bar arm ride.

Review all maneuvers, 4–10, for check-out in next lesson.

10. Double arm lock and roll.

Review all maneuvers for check out in next lesson.

Scrimmage from double arm lock and roll pinning position (four 15-sec. periods).

Scoring: One point for keeping bottom man on his back or one point if bottom man gets out of pinning situation.

LESSON IX

Warm-up: review all maneuvers for check-out.

Check out #1 (see marking system explanation in Appendix).

4. Sit-out and turn-in to crawfish.
5. Escape to neutral from half nelson pin and crawfish to top.
6. Escape from reverse nelson pin.
7. Release for tight waist ride.
8. Release for bar arm and outside crotch.
9. Block near-side half nelson with elbow-lock roll to key lock.
10. Double arm lock and roll.

LESSON X

Warm-up: spinning.

11. Breakdowns
    a. Tight waist and near-arm pull.
    b. Far-ankle and near-arm pull.
    c. Crotch pry and near-arm pull.

Spinning with breakdowns.

Review double arm lock and roll.

12. Knee tap as a counter for double underhooks.

Scrimmage from double underhook position (four 20-sec. periods).

Scoring: Two points for takedown and maintaining control in the top position.

LESSON XI

Warm-up: review spinning with breakdowns.

Review knee tap counter for double underhooks.

13. Far-side roll to reverse nelson and cradle pin.

Sit-out, turn-in, side-roll sequence II(3) and (13).

Scrimmage from referee's position on the mat (four 30-sec. periods). Return to starting position after each escape or reversal.

Scoring: Escape 1 point, reversal 2 points, pin 5 points. (Only top man can score on pin.)

LESSON XII

Warm-up: spinning and breakdowns.

Review far-side roll to reverse nelson and cradle pin.

Review sit-out, turn-in, side-roll sequence.

14. Inside crotch pry and arm pull to bar arm and helf nelson pin.

Competition 1. Olympic ground wrestling with standing prohibited (see competition schedule and score sheet in Appendix).

(1) Instructions
    a. Match will be for two periods of 1 minute each.
    b. Use NCAA start from referee's position on mat.
    c. Odd numbered men are on top the first period and the positions are reversed for the second period, with the even numbered men on top.
    d. After each escape, reversal, or stand-up, the bottom man returns to the underneath position.
    e. Points are awarded for each change of position and near-fall as follows: escape, 1; reversal, 2; near-fall, 3; predicament, 1.
    f. A fall terminates a period. Only the top man may score a fall, and it should be recorded on the score sheet with the elapsed time. A fall occurs when the shoulder blades are held in contact with the mat for two seconds.
    g. Pairings: Size off by weights and count off by fours. First matches: ones vs. twos with threes and fours as referees. Second matches: threes vs. fours with ones and twos as referees.

(2) Instructions for referees (NCAA Guide, Rule 13) and referee's signals.
    a. Face wrestlers at start of match.
    b. Commands: Say "Stop" to stop match for out-of-bounds escapes, reversals, and stand-ups. To resume wrestling, bring to center of mat in referee's position and say, "ready," as preparatory command, and "wrestle," as command of execution.
    c. Call out the points as they are scored.
    d. Get head down on mat to see near-falls and falls.
    e. Maintain control and stay in command of match.
    f. Prohibit illegal holds: twisting hammer lock, front head lock, straight head scissors, over scissors, flying mare with palm up, double arm bar with hands locked, full nelson, strangle holds, unnecessary roughness, all slams, toe holds, twisting knee lock, bending or twisting or forcing the head or any limb or joint beyond normal limits of movement, holds for punishment alone, pulling back thumb or less than four fingers (NCAA Guide, Rule 10, Secs. 1 to 6).
    g. Prohibit technical violations: interlocking hands or arms around body or legs, holding leg or legs with both hands or arms, grasping clothing, stalling, delaying the match, intentional going off mat (NCAA Guide, Rule 10, Sec. 7).

LESSON XIII

Discuss competition in preceding lesson and point out the common errors. Review sit-out, turn-in, side-roll sequence. Review inside crotch pry and arm pull to bar arm and half nelson pin.

15. Counter sit-out and turn-in with overdrag.
16. Snapdown and spin behind.

Scrimmage from referee's position on the mat (NCAA Guide, Rules 7, 8 and 9). (Four 30-sec. periods.)

NCAA rules except prohibit standing. Continuous match for 30 seconds.
   Scoring: Escape, 1 point; reversal, 2 points; go behind, 2 points; predicament, 1 point; near-fall, 3 points; fall, 5 points (NCAA Guide, Rules 8 and 9).

LESSON XIV

Warm-up: review all maneuvers for check-out in next lesson.
17. Sit-out and turn out.

Scrimmage from referee's position on mat (four 30-sec. periods). NCAA rules except prohibit standing.
Scoring: same as in Lesson XIII.
Individual review for any who are having difficulty.

LESSON XV

Individual informal review as class assembles. Review sit-out, turn-out, Check-out #2.

11. Breakdowns: (a) tight waist (b), far ankle (c), crotch pry.
12. Knee tap as counter for double underhooks.
13. Far-side roll to reverse nelson and cradle pin.
14. Inside crotch pry and arm pull to bar arm and half nelson pin.
15. Counter sit-out and turn-in with overdrag.
16. Snapdown and spin behind.
17. Sit-out, and turn-out.

Sequence: sit-out, turn-in, side-roll sequence. Individual informal review for any who had difficulty.

LESSON XVI

Warm-up: spinning drill.
Review sit-out and turn-out. Add turn-in when turn-out is blocked.
18. Switch to two-on-one bar arm.
19. Two-on-one bar arm ride and release for it.
21. Overhook and hip throw from underneath to reverse nelson pin.

Scrimmage: Start in two-on-one bar arm ride position (four 30-sec. periods).
NCAA rules except prohibit standing.
   Scoring: Escape, 1; reversal, 2; go behind, 2; near-fall, 2; fall, 5; maintaining top for 30 sec., 1 point; predicament, 1.

LESSON XVII

Warm-up: review escapes from half nelson and reverse nelson pins.

Review sit-out, turn-out, turn-in, side-roll sequence.

Review switch.

Review escape from two-on-one bar arm ride.

Review overhook and hip throw from underneath to reverse nelson pin.

20. Switch sequence (first four maneuvers). Attempt switch turn-in, side roll, roll-through.

22. Near-leg pick-up and forward trip against stand-up to all fours.

Scrimmage: Start in referee's position on the mat (2 one-minute periods).

NCAA rules, except prohibit standing.

Scoring: escape, 1; reversal, 2; go behind, 2; predicament, 1; near-fall, 3; fall, 5; maintaining top for one minute, 1 point.

LESSON XVIII

Warm-up: switch sequence through re-roll and right-handed switch.

20. Switch sequence. Add reswitch, left-handed switch, lock arm, and spin across to key lock.

Review near-leg pick-up and forward trip.

23. Near-leg pick-up and backward drop.

Competition 2. Start in referee's position on the mat.

Two one-minute periods. NCAA rules, prohibit standing.

Organize as in Lesson XII.

Scoring: escape, 1; reversal, 2; go behind, 2; near-fall, 3; predicament, 1; fall (record on score sheet with elapsed time). The fall terminates the period and either contestant may score a fall. If each contestant gains a fall, the quickest fall wins.

LESSON XIX

Warm-up: review entire switch sequence.

Review near-leg pick-up and backward drop.

24. Tight waist and head pry to hammer lock and half nelson.

26. Back heel from rear standing.

Discuss competition in preceding lesson and point out the common errors.

Scrimmage from referee's position on mat (four 30-sec. periods). NCAA rules as in Lesson XVIII. Permit standing in rear-standing position. No standing in neutral position. Stay on knees.

LESSON XX

Warm-up: switch sequence for time. (Give plus check for 5 seconds or less.)

Review tight waist and head pry.

25. Block head pry.

Review back heel from rear standing.

27. Switch to counter back heel.

Scrimmage: same as for Lesson XIX.

Practice switch sequence informally to both sides. Announce check-out for
next lesson.

LESSON XXI

Warm-up: informal practice of switch sequence both sides.
Time switch sequence both sides. Plus check for 5 seconds or under.
Review switch to counter back heel. Check-out #3.
18. Switch to two-on-one bar arm.
19. Release two-on-one bar arm.
21. Overhook and hip throw from underneath to reverse nelson pin.
22. Near-leg pick-up and forward trip.
23. Near-leg pick-up and backward drop.
24. Tight waist and head pry to hammer lock and half nelson.
25. Block head pry.
26. Back heel from rear standing.
27. Switch to counter back heel.

LESSON XXII

Warm-up: informal practice of switch sequence and individual time
check for anyone wanting to try it.
28. Stand-up escape.
29. Crawfish reversal.
Scrimmage: same as for Lesson XIX.

LESSON XXIII

Warm-up: spinning with breakdowns.
Review stand-up escape. Review crawfish reversal.
30. Cross-face against single leg hold.
    A. Step over and lock near leg.
    B. Far-arm and near-ankle to arm lock and body lock pin.
31. Stand-up against cross-face.
    Spinning with cross-face and stand up.

LESSON XXIV

Warm-up: spinning with breakdowns and cross-face.
Review cross-face against single leg hold, both (a) and (b).
32. Release far ankle and sit out.
33. Double leg tackle to half nelson cradle.
Scrimmage from referee's position on mat (two one-minute periods). NCAA
rules. Stand-ups and take-downs permitted.
Scoring: escape, 1; reversal, 2; take-down, 2; near fall, 3; predicament, 1.

LESSON XXV

Warm-up: spinning with breakdowns and cross-face.
Review release for far ankle and sit-out.

Review double leg tackle to half nelson cradle.

34. Counter side-head lock with backward drop.

35. Arm drag counter against single leg pick-up.

Scrimmage for take-downs (one 2-minute period). Start from neutral position on feet and return to neutral position after each take-down. Score two points for each take-down.

LESSON XXVI

Warm-up: switch sequence.

Review arm-drag counter against single leg pick-up.

Review counter side-head lock with backward drop.

36. Underarm sneak.

Scrimmage: NCAA rules and scoring (one 2-minute period for takedowns). Four 30-sec. periods on the mat). Announce check-out for next lesson.

LESSON XXVII

Warm-up: informal review for check-out.

Check-out #4.

28. Stand-up escape.

29. Crawfish reversal.

30. Cross-face (A and B).

31. Stand-up against cross-face.

32. Release far ankle and sit-out.

33. Double leg tackle to half nelson cradle.

34. Counter side-head lock with backward drop.

35. Arm drag counter against single leg pick-up.

Review underarm sneak.

Scrimmage: NCAA rules, starting in neutral position on feet. One 2-minute period of continuous wrestling.

LESSON XXVIII

Warm-up: spinning with breakdowns and cross-face.

Review arm-drag counter against single leg pick-up sequence.

Review underarm sneak.

Competition 3. NCAA rules (three 1-minute periods. Size off and count off by 4's):

   1 vs. 2; 3, referee; 4, keep score.   3 vs. 4; 1, referee; 2, keep score.

LESSON XXIX

Warm-up: check out make-ups and informal practice.

Discuss competition in preceding lesson and point out common errors.

Drill on the maneuvers that need more practice or introduce.

37. Stretcher.

Competition 4. Same as Lesson XXVIII.

    1 vs. 4; 2, referee; 3, keep score.   2 vs. 3; 3, referee; 1, keep score.

LESSON XXX

Warm-up: check out make-ups and informal practice.

Discuss competition in previous lesson and point out common errors.

Drill on maneuvers that need more practice or introduce.

38. Cross-body ride to guillotine.

Competition 5. Same as Lesson XXVIII.

    1 vs. 3; 2, referee; 4, keep score.   2 vs. 4; 1, referee; 3, keep score.

Appendix

SYMBOLS FOR MARKING ATTENDANCE

In order that each instructor's attendance and grade book may be interpreted, all instructors employ the following symbols to indicate each student's attendance, absence, or tardiness:

✓ Present	⊖ Excused absence
O Absent	⊕ Present but excused
◐ Tardy	⊕ Made-up absence

GRADING POLICY

One unexcused absence, no penalty.

Two unexcused absences, final grade reduced one-half letter; i.e., from B— to C+.

Three unexcused absences, final grade reduced one letter; i.e., from B to C.

Unexcused absences for more than 10 per cent of class meeting, automatic failure.

No student who misses more than 30 per cent of the total class periods (whether excused or unexcused) can receive credit for a skills and techniques course.

MARKING SYSTEM

CHECK-OUTS.   50 per cent of final mark.

1. **Procedure.**   Everyone starts with a mark of 85. Any deviation from average class performance in the measurable elements will be noted in the class roll book by a series of check symbols which will effect the mark of 85 as follows:

Inferior performance, mark a minus check " — ". Subtract two for each minus check.

Very inferior performance, mark a double minus check " = ". Subtract four for each double minus check.

	CLASS ROLL BOOK CHECK OUT CHART																																85	MARK
	CHECK OUT #1					CHECK OUT #2							CHECK OUT #3											CHECK OUT #4									
NAMES	4	5	6	7	8	9	10	11	12	13	14	15	16	17	18	19	20	21	22	23	24	25	26	27	28	29	30	31	32	33	34	35	±	

Complete lack of ability or unexcused absence, mark a zero "0". Subtract six for each zero mark.

Outstanding performance, mark a plus check " + ". Add two for each plus check.

Superior performance, mark a double plus check "++". Add four for each double-plus check.

2. Measurable Elements. Check daily any deviation above or below average.
    a. Attitudes and interest (workmanship, responsibility, and industry).
    b. Competence (periodic check-outs of skill in maneuvers and sequences).
    c. Leadership (refereeing, recording matches, and teaching).

COMPETITION. 50 per cent of final mark.

1. Each student is scheduled for five matches against opponents as near his weight and ability as possible. (See competition schedule and score sheet.)
2. A cumulative rating (see competition record card) is maintained for each student on the basis of the result of each match in accordance with the following scoring system.
3. Scoring system for recording each match:

    Win fall, +5.   Lose fall, —5.
    Win decision, +3.   Lose decision, —3.
    Draw, —1 for each contestant.
    Win by default due to accidental injury, +3.
    Lose by default due to accidental injury, 0.
    Win by default due to injury from illegal hold, +5.
    Lose by default due to injury from illegal hold, —5.
    Excused from competition, 0.

Date_____

Competition Schedule and Score Sheet

Recording Instructions:

Match Scoring   POINTS:
Takedown   2
Escape   1
Reversal   2
Near Falls   3
Predicament   1
PINS:
Write "pin" and the time for it in the column under the period in which it occurs and opposite the man's name who gained the pin. Also write "pin" in the last column opposite the winner's name.

DEFAULTS:
If contestant is injured and unable to continue write "injured" in appropriate column and also in the total score column. Also indicate whether injury was due to an "accident" or "illegal hold".

MATCH NO.		CONTESTANTS	PERIODS			SCORE OR
			1	2	3	PIN
I	1	NAME				
		NUMBER				
		WEIGHT				
	2	NAME				
		NUMBER				
		WEIGHT				
II	3	NAME				
		NUMBER				
		WEIGHT				
	4	NAME				
		NUMBER				
		WEIGHT				
III	5	NAME				
		NUMBER				
		WEIGHT				
	6	NAME				
		NUMBER				
		WEIGHT				
IV	7	NAME				
		NUMBER				
		WEIGHT				
	8	NAME				
		NUMBER				

```
┌─────────────────────────────────────────────────────────────────────────────┐
│              SPRINGFIELD COLLEGE, MASSACHUSETTS        NO.___                  │
│                                                                               │
│     INDIVIDUAL RECORD CARD                                                     │
│     WRESTLING COMPETITION_____ TO_____                       │
│                                                                               │
│  No.   Sec.   Name    Matches   1   2   3   4   5   6   7   Grade             │
└─────────────────────────────────────────────────────────────────────────────┘
```

No.	Sec.	Name	Matches	1	2	3	4	5	6	7	Grade
Wt. ___	___		Opp.								
			Result								
			Rate								
Wt. ___	___		Opp.								
			Result								
			Rate								

Each man gains a fall: fastest, +2; slowest, −2.

Unexcused absence, −5.

4. Record of competition:

   Each competitor's score is recorded on the competition record card after each match. His rating is then computed and this rating is used for scheduling his next match against an opponent equal in rating and weight.

5. Evaluation of the competition:

   The cumulative score on the competition record card is the sum of all the match scores and is the rating used to determine the competition mark from the following chart.

6. Chart for transforming the cumulative competition score into a mark for the competition.

   If the rate is a plus number, the mark is located in the top row above the rate number. If the rate is a minus number, the mark is located in the bottom row below the rate number.

Mark For Plus Rate	75	76	77	78	79	80	81	82	83	84	85	86	87	88	89	90	91	92	93	94	95	96	97	98	99	100
Rate ±	0	1	2	3	4	5	6	7	8	9	10	11	12	13	14	15	16	17	18	19	20	21	22	23	24	25
Mark For Minus Rate	75	74	73	72	71	70	69	68	67	66	65	64	63	62	61	60	59	58	57	56	55	54	53	52	51	50

7. *Final Mark:* The competition and check-out marks are averaged and the numerical mark is converted to a letter mark as follows:

A+, 97–99	B+, 87–89	C+, 77–79
A , 93–96	B , 83–86	C , 73–76
A−, 90–92	B−, 80–82	C−, 70–72
D+, 67–69	F, below 60	
D , 63–66	I, incomplete	
D−, 60–62		

SELECTED BIBLIOGRAPHY

AMATEUR ATHLETIC UNION. *A.A.U. Wrestling Guide.* New York: Amateur Athletic Union. Annual. Official rules and record book of A.A.U. and international wrestling.

AMERICAN ASSOCIATION FOR HEALTH, PHYSICAL EDUCATION AND RECREATION. *Physical Education for High School Students.* Washington, D.C.: A.A.H.P.E.R., 1955. Pp. 307-32.

GALLAGHER, EDWIN C., and PEERY, REX. *Wrestling.* New York: The Ronald Press Co., 1951.

KEEN, C. P., SPEIDEL, C. M., and SWARTZ, R. H. *Championship Wrestling.* Annapolis, Md.: U.S. Naval Institute, 1958.

KENNEY, HAROLD E., and LAW, GLENN C. *Wrestling.* New York: McGraw-Hill Book Co., Inc., 1952.

NATIONAL COLLEGIATE ATHLETIC ASSOCIATION. *N.C.A.A. Wrestling Guide.* New York: National Collegiate Athletic Bureau. Annual. Official rules and record book of collegiate and scholastic wrestling.

PERRY, REX, and UMBACH, ARNOLD W. *Wrestling Instructor's Guide.* Chicago: The Athletic Institute, 1956.

STONE, HENRY A. *Wrestling Intercollegiate and Olympic.* Englewood Cliffs, N.J.: Prentice-Hall, Inc., 1950.

UMBACH, ARNOLD W., and JOHNSON, WARREN R. *Successful Wrestling: Its Basis and Problems.* St. Louis: The C. V. Mosby Co., 1953.

American Wrestling Coaches and Officials Association Periodicals:

Amateur Wrestling News. Excellent coverage of amateur wrestling, published 16 times a year during the wrestling season.

Mentor. Published monthly except June and July, with a wrestling section in each issue.

A Bibliography of Amateur Wrestling (A.W.C.O.A., Committee on Extension of Wrestling). Provides a complete and up-to-date list of books, periodical articles, theses, films and filmstrips, syllabuses, charts, and unpublished materials on amateur wrestling.

Index